WORLD WAR II

igloobooks

igloobooks

Published in 2016
by Igloo Books Ltd
Cottage Farm
Sywell
NN6 0BJ
www.igloobooks.com

LEO002 1016
2 4 6 8 10 9 7 5 3 1
ISBN 978-1-78670-260-9

Cover image: Johncairns / © Getty Images

Cover designed by Simon Parker
Edited by Jasmin Peppiatt

Written by Gerard Cheshire

Printed and manufactured in China

Contents

Introduction

By the time World War I had reached its bloody conclusion, many felt that the world had changed for good. A generation of men had perished. Many countries stood impoverished and bitter new enmities had emerged. In Eastern Europe a new and unknown political system had sprouted in the form of communism, the alien nature of which caused fear around the rest of the world. In Central Europe, new countries had been formed from broken off pieces of old Empires. The new states of Yugoslavia and Czechoslovakia brought new opportunities and also fresh tensions. In the USA the period after World War I was a time of substantial growth and development as it became the largest economy in the world.

At the Paris Peace Conference of 1919, 32 nations met to discuss how peace could be maintained in future and this kind of bloody conflict avoided for all time. Of all the decisions taken in Paris, one, later called the War Guilt Clause, required Germany to 'accept the responsibility of Germany and her allies for causing all the loss and damage' of the war. It forced Germany to disarm, make territorial concessions and pay massive reparations to the countries of the Entente.

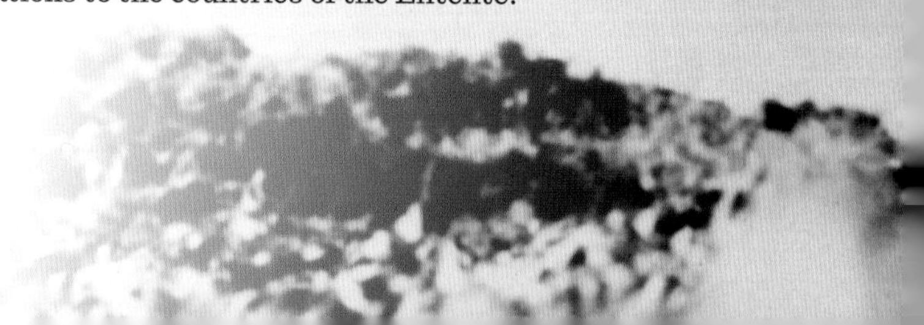

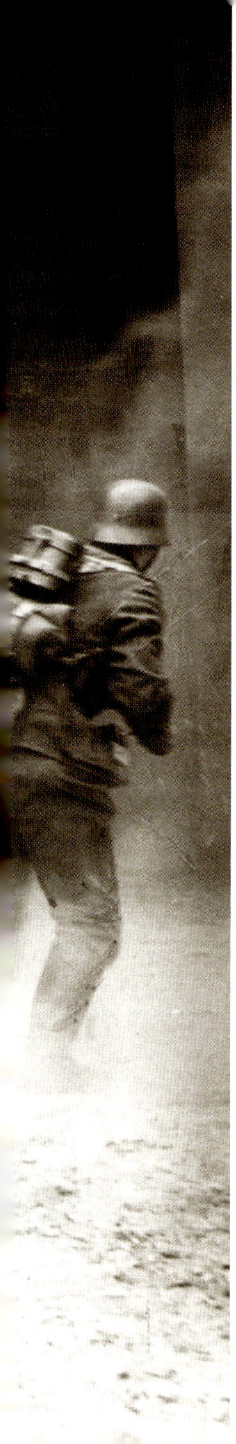

The War Guilt Clause was intended to maintain peace for all, but instead sowed the seeds for further, even more extensive war, just twenty years later.

Embittered and in penury, the ordinary German people began to seek a saviour and a decade after World War 1 they found one in the shape of Adolf Hitler. After a rapid rise to fame and a surge in popular support, Hitler became Chancellor of Germany in 1933 on a manifesto of German racial supremacy and aggressive nationalism. His Nazi party left the League of Nations in 1933 and from that moment onwards the country was preparing for war on a huge scale. German industry went into overdrive building weapons and technology and a new army was recruited and trained.

Hitler's aim was to make Germany the ruler of Europe. His fanatical nationalism led him to believe he had a right to invade other countries, occupy their space and control the race and nature of their populations to match his own beliefs. But he could not have done it alone. The seeds of hatred he spread around him found fertile ground in a nation that was beaten, bitter and humiliated. Ironically, the evil beliefs of the Nazi party came from decisions intended to maintain peace forever.

German soldiers using flamethrowers against a French bunker on the Maginot Line, 1940

WORLD WAR TWO

A news boy selling the News Of The World carries a poster proclaiming Britain's declaration of war on Germany, 1939

An American soldier from 7th Armored Division mans the machine gun of his tank while on manoeuvres, 1942

Troops from the 48th Royal Marines at Saint-Aubin-sur-mer on Juno Beach, Normandy, France, during the D-Day landings, 6th June 1944

祝日獨伊防共協

Bellicose Bullies

Had Germany and Japan invested more time and effort into empire building over the eighteenth and nineteenth centuries, then they may not have felt the need to 'catch up' as Empires by quite such brutal means. Instead of negotiating access to worldwide resources the subtle way, over centuries, by colonizing second and third world populations, they found themselves wanting. So, lacking the skills of diplomacy that are learnt and honed by experience of long-term empire administration, both Germany and Japan decided to go about it the aggressive way. Like the playground bully, they opted to steal from those who had won it. As we all know, bullies may succeed initially by pushing around and intimidating, but sooner or later the victims rally support and pin the bullies against the wall.

Flags of the allies Japan, Germany and Italy on the building of Japan's leading newspaper 'Tokyo Yomiuri', Japan, December 3rd 1937

Prior to the early twentieth century, Japan had been very inward looking. Culturally, the Japanese had developed a suspicion of the outside world because they were an island nation and felt vulnerable to invasion and conquest. If we draw a parallel with the British Isles, it is interesting to note that invasion and conquest is exactly what made the British so different from the Japanese. British horizons were widened by the flux resulting from the overlay of new peoples, which is why the British were so good at empire building.

Opportunism combined with ambiguous cultural identity allowed the British to ambitiously exploit resources across the globe. Meanwhile, the Japanese grew evermore culturally blinkered and disinclined towards international enterprise.

The Germans had a similarly paranoid way of viewing the world to the Japanese, but for different reasons. Quite apart from being an island nation, Germany had very little coastline. Instead, it had borders with a number of other European populations, which made it feel vulnerable to attack.

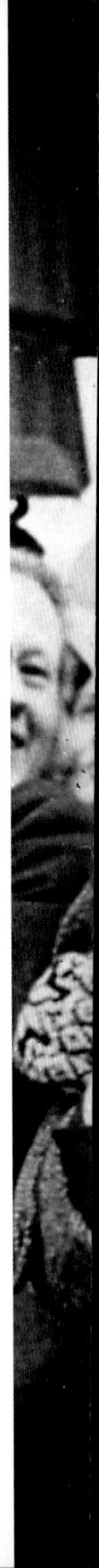

Crowd cheering Matsuoka Yosuke, Japanese Foreign Secretary, during a visit in Berlin, 1939

"LET US
GO FORWARD
TOGETHER"

To make matters worse, the Germans had already tried to rampage their way to a larger territory with World War I, only to suffer defeat by spreading themselves too thin when the Allies had inexhaustible colonial resources at hand.
But Germany's resentment at being put in its place, by peoples it wanted to believe were inferior, had only given it the resolve to try again.

Let Us Go Forward Together
(Churchill) an iconic WWII poster

The Axis

The term 'Axis' was used by the Allies to describe the enemy nations in World War II because Germany, Austria and Italy formed a central line of axis running north to south, dividing Europe in two. The term remained in use when Japan allied with Germany as a matter of convenience.

Vidkun Quisling, Norwegian fascist politician who collaborated with the Axis powers during World War Two

Adolf Hitler arrives at a military parade for the celebration of his 50th birthday on April 20, 1939

IA-148764

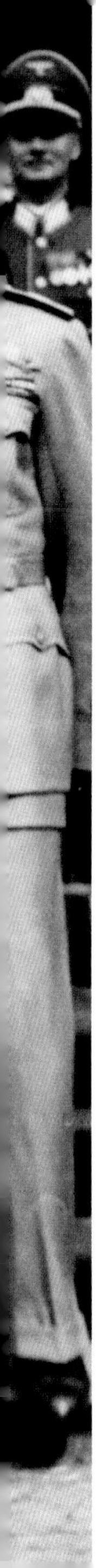

What Germany and Japan had in common was their delusion of superiority towards other races which, as any psychologist will tell you, is actually an expression of insecurity and inferiority. In the case of Germany, the primary targets of prejudice were Jews and other peoples who were not Aryan.

They also had disdain for any societies, cultures and politics that clashed with Nazi ideals and nations that were not Teutonic. In addition, they had quasi-Darwinian notions about racial purity and perfection, which prompted them to purge their own population of individuals with physical and mental disabilities.

The Japanese cultivated particular hatred for the Chinese, because they were the traditional enemy across the sea. Their culture included unquestioning reverence for their Emperor, whom they believed was a living god, and this allowed them to believe that they were a divine race. In turn, this gave the Japanese a quasi-Darwinian understanding of strength, which meant that most were prepared to fight to the death as a matter of honour. This furnished them with a marked disdain for enemy forces that were prepared to surrender, rather than fight to the end.

A meeting of leaders of the Axis powers in Germany (front row, left to right) Hermann Goering, Benito Mussolini, Adolf Hitler and Count Galeazzo Ciano, 1932

As both Germany and Japan had very clear delusions of racial supremacy, they would have loathed one another had they not had political reason to become allies. It was in both of their interests to ally because their geographical separation meant that enemy forces would need to be divided, to effectively fight two wars. This was an attractive proposition, as both were well aware that the Central Powers of World War I had ultimately lost the war due to attrition of finite resources against an enemy able to source further resources. The fundamental strategy, common to both Germany and Japan, was to capture new resources and utilize them along the way, thereby preventing attrition from becoming a determining factor and allowing both nations to permanently secure new territories.

German chancellor Adolf Hitler (left) and Italian dictator Benito Mussolini in jovial mood during a drive through the streets of Florence, Italy, 1938

Bewildered investors mill about at Wall Street, New York, after the Stock Market collapse on 'Black Friday', October 1929

The Great Depression

In October 1929, the Wall Street Crash occurred in the USA, marking the beginning of the Great Depression. Germany had been loaned large sums of money by the Americans following World War I, due to the cost of having to rebuild its economy. After the Wall Street Crash, the Americans had no choice but to call in the monies owed to it and gave Germany ninety days to begin repaying. The knock-on effect of this was to cause amplified inflation in Germany. The value of money dropped so rapidly that it wasn't worth the paper it was printed on and the German population suffered extreme hardship as a result.

At the time, Adolf Hitler was already leader of the Nazi party in Germany and he used the Depression to his advantage by whipping the nation into a frenzied desire for social reform. He was in the right place at the right time, as it didn't take much to sell the idea of a Germany reborn as a European power to be reckoned with. Having captured his people's imagination, the foundations were laid for Hitler's rise to power. The establishment disliked Hitler and did their level best to prevent Germany from falling under his spell, but by 1933 the nation was on the verge of civil war, such was the divide in opinion about how to stage the German recovery.

On January 30th Hitler became Chancellor, much to Hindenburg's indignation, who famously called him "the little corporal" alluding to the true nature of his personality. Under Hitler's leadership the nation then rallied to deliver the promise of renewed German might.

For Japan, the Great Depression had a different though no less significant impact. The Japanese economy had been very reliant on the trade of luxury goods in exchange for natural resources, which it lacked. When the financial slump impacted the world, Japan suddenly found that other nations drew back their purse strings. Japan's export trade fell by fifty percent and things looked bleak. Soon afterwards, in 1931, Japan invaded Manchurian China, to access resources and provision itself with territory in which to build and house its expanding population. A military dictatorship came to power, with Emperor Hirohito as its figurehead, and the stage was set for the further expansion of the new Japanese Empire that was to follow.

Both Germany and Japan responded to the Great Depression by nurturing and then implementing designs on neighbouring territories to access the resources they needed. They saw it as a necessary means to an end, while other nations disagreed, and so the world went to war for the second time.

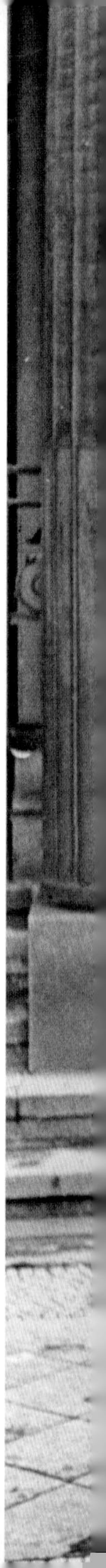

The Berlin Stock Exchange remains shut as a result of the closing of the London Exchange during the Great Depression in the United Kingdom, Monday 21st September 1931

Japanese troops marching through Shanghai, 1937

An American aircraft continues on its flight after dropping ammunition by parachutes to waiting Chinese in their fight against the Japanese

Adolf Hitler and his staff salute the teams during the opening ceremonies of the XI Olympic Games in August 1936 in Berlin, Germany

The Build-up to War

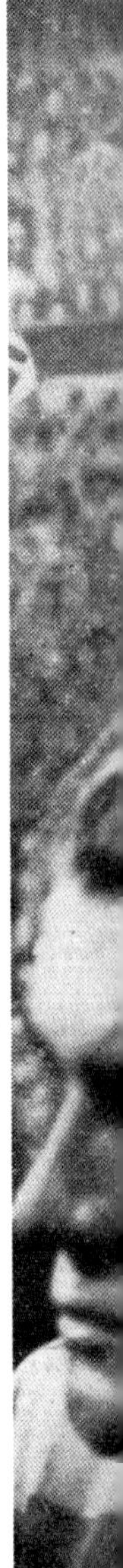

In the years preceding World War II it was evident that Germany had military ambitions, simply because of the rhetoric used by Adolf Hitler. There was also a considerable increase in the manufacture of arms and machines of war, as well as the active recruitment of young men into the Nazi Party and German forces.

However, politicians in other European countries had the naïve idea that avoiding conflict was a matter of diplomacy. They invested a great deal of time and effort into visiting Hitler, thinking that he would be swayed by their good will. In fact, they were making the mistake of judging him by their own standards, for the truth was that Hitler had every intention of putting his plans of conquest into action regardless of these gestures. He was merely pulling the wool over their eyes as he prepared for all-out warfare. When the time was right, Hitler simply got on with what he had always intended, confident that nothing and no one could stop him.

A similar situation had arisen in Japan. There too, military resources were being amassed to set the wheels of territorial ambition in motion.

Nazi party members listening to a speech by Hitler, 1930

Hitler baut auf
Helft mit
Kauft deutsche
Ware

With the Japanese Emperor on the throne, the regime itself didn't need a particular personality to take the lead, but the intent was clear. As the Japanese already had a foothold in Manchuria, they had a pre-prepared platform from which to launch their campaign.

Germany's first move was to annex an area of territory in 1938, known a Sudetenland, which was home to German speaking populations in Czechoslovakia.

Then, in 1939, the Germans prepared to invade Poland for the purpose of expanding the German living space. The British warned Germany that war would be declared if the Germans set foot in Poland, so Hitler duly instructed his army to encroach Polish territory on September 1st. Britain declared war on Germany two days later on September 3rd. As the Germans moved into Poland from the west, the Russians invaded Poland from the east as a counter measure, fearful of Hitler's underlying ambitions.

The Japanese began the second phase of their invasion of China in 1937 by capturing Beijing. They then progressively took further swathes of territory.

German propaganda poster from 1934 reads 'Help Hitler Build – Buy German Products'

German troops remove the border barrier between Poland and Germany during the invasion of Poland, 1939

This was known as the Second Sino-Japanese War, and Japan did not enter World War II until 1940 when it joined the Axis, having invaded the colony of French Indo-China, which is now known as Vietnam.

A newspaper seller carries a hoarding pronouncing the declaration of war between Britain and Germany, 1939

A crowd gathered to listen as Prime Minister Benito Mussolini declares war on Britain and France, 1940

The Political Map

Before World War II, Germany annexed Austria, making it part of German territory. This, together with Bulgaria, Romania, Italy and Hungary, formed the Axis powers. The Italian leader, Benito Mussolini, was an ardent admirer of Hitler. In 1941, Japan also joined the Axis Powers.

To begin with, the European Allies comprised the United Kingdom, France and Poland, but many other nations were drawn in on the Allies' side as the war progressed, including Russia, China, USA, Canada, Brazil, Mexico, Australia, New Zealand and South Africa.

As the war moved into 1940 and then into 1941, the political map evolved as the Axis powers invaded new territories. Some conquered nations resisted occupation, while others dealt with their lot by cooperating, for the sake of survival. A number of European colonies in Asia and Southeast-Asia had become more autonomous under Japanese occupation and resisted having to return to colonial control when they were liberated.

A member of the French Resistance, taking cover behind truck from a German sniper during fight

The flags of Fascist Italy and Nazi Germany flying together, 1937

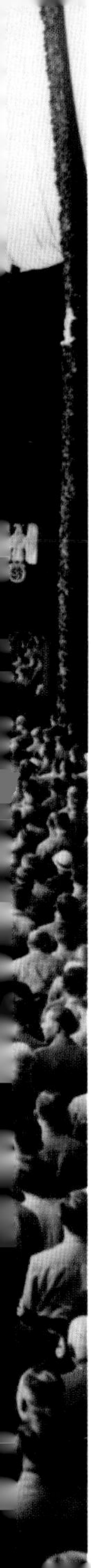

Although Russia was on the side of the Allies, it had its own agenda too. While most of the Allies were mainly interested in defeating the Axis and restoring the political map, the Russians saw an opportunity to seize eastern European territories and enlarge their territory into other Slavic nations.

The motive behind this was communism. Stalin and his comrades had the vision of a modern world dominated by their particular brand of dictatorial communism, so they wanted the political map to include as much red as possible to enable the spread of communist ideas and influence.

A few nations were independent in their intentions, such as Finland. In effect, it fought its own war, as it battled both the Russians and the Germans. Geographically, Finland was strategically advantageous to invade, providing generous access to the Baltic Sea, but the Finns had no desire to be occupied by either one of the opposed forces.

Nuremberg Rally, 1934

Motivation

The motives for World War I were largely to do with political ideas of pride and honour amongst the ruling classes. This lent itself, very much, to the overriding feeling that millions had lost their lives pointlessly in the aftermath of the war. Fundamentally, the European nations belonged to a shared ideological mind-set. This is why, for example, it was possible for German and British troops to down their weapons and share Christmas together as they did in 1914. This demonstrated clearly that there was a sense that they were only fighting because they had been told to by their superiors. It also expressed an acceptance of subordination and class hierarchy, because that is all people knew at the time.

British and German troops make a Christmas and New Year truce in the trenches of the Western Front, 1915

A smiling member of the female branch of the Hitler Youth, carrying a collecting tin, circa 1938

Baut
Jugendherbergen
und Heime

World War II was different in this regard, as European class structures had been eroded, so that people were no longer naïve enough to risk death for no real reason. However, people were willing to fight for an ideological cause, and this is what they got. The Nazi regime had conditioned many Germans into believing they were a master race, destined to rule Europe, so Hitler had a devoted army who willingly obeyed his every command. Although this worked in Hitler's favour, by generating cohesion in the German population and making them a formidable force, it also worked against him because the Allies were able to use propaganda to motivate their own peoples against the Germans.

The Nazis quickly made a reputation for themselves as brutal, merciless killers because they had been conditioned to think of other populations as inferior. This played into the hands of Allied governments, because they were able to portray Germans as evil. The Germans were 'baddies', while the Allies were the 'goodies'. Needless to say, the Germans didn't think of themselves as evil, but rather that they had an inalienable right to rise to power and put other humans in their place. So, it was this ideological disparity that underpinned and incentivized both the Germans and the Allies.

German dictator Adolf Hitler takes the salute at a Nazi parade in Germany

The Japanese had a similar reputation as cruel and inhuman in their treatment of other peoples, because they too had the idea that they were a superior race. The notion that large areas of the world might end up being controlled by the Nazi and Japanese regimes was made even more unacceptable by this perception of evil intent among the Allies that an absolute determination arose to defeat the Axis at any cost, for the sake of restoring the world to a place of relative goodwill.

A member of the Hitler Youth with a swastika flag at a Nazi rally in Germany

The Blitzkrieg

Following Germany's invasion of Poland, resulting in the British declaration of war, there was a fallow period of inaction, now known as the Phony War, lasting just over eight months. During this time, Hitler was sizing up the enemy and allowing their forces to become complacent with boredom. He made gestures suggesting that he was hoping they may acquiesce and allow him to keep Poland, but it transpired that he was amassing a large military force ready to invade France and the Lowlands.

When the offensive was implemented it caught the Allied forces by surprise. The Germans struck so hard and fast that there was little the opposing forces could do except retreat and attempt to slow down the Nazi advance.

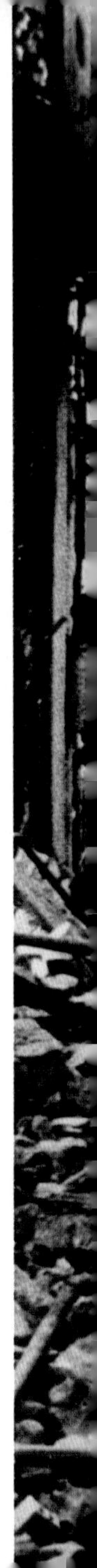

A scene typical of many French towns in northern France with destruction and chaos everywhere following Germany's victory in France in 1940

The Germans had introduced a new mode of warfare called Blitzkrieg (Lightning-War). It was designed to be swift and overwhelming, rather like a tsunami, so that resistance was futile. A German officer, named Heinz Guderian had developed the concept in the early 1930s by optimizing tank design along with that of armoured cars and artillery, so that they were highly effective at moving rapidly over rough terrain.

He had also fully equipped the tanks and military units with radios, so that communication was state-of-the-art and efficient. As the tanks forged their way forwards, blasting any key opposition units out of action, they were followed by crack divisions of storm troopers, who dealt with the enemy troops while they were still in a state of disarray. To the rear, artillery would be instructed to take out any enemy positions inaccessible to the tanks.

German troops entering Poland after a 'blitzkrieg'

The spearhead of the Blitzkrieg emerged from the Ardennes forest on the 10th May, 1940 and proved unstoppable as it widened and continued westward. Another advantage of its rapid progress was that the Allies were unable to relocate and deploy forces from elsewhere to impede the Blitzkrieg. Added to that, the Allies' equipment was inferior and they had a different strategic mind-set, so they were outgunned and outmanoeuvred. To avoid being killed or being taken captive, the Allies had no choice but to make a rapid tactical retreat and figure out what to do next.

An important factor in the success of the Blitzkrieg was air support. The German air force, the Luftwaffe, was very effective at dive-bombing Allied columns and strategically bombing installations farther afield. This had the effect of weakening supply lines and softening targets to enable the offensive to continue unabated. All in all, the Germans had devised a war machine, which the Allies were unable to counter at that stage of the war, thereby allowing the Germans territorial purchase on mainland Europe.

German soldiers going on the attack on the Western Front in France, 1940

New Race to the Sea

During the opening stages of World War I, the Allies had been successful in preventing the Germans from reaching the coast of France and Belgium. When it came to World War II, the Allies were not so fortunate. When they realized that the German forces could not be stopped it put a whole new complexion on the situation at hand. The British decided that the best plan of action was to use the sea to their advantage and organize a mass evacuation, thereby leaving the Germans on the coast.

The point of evacuation was to be a small French town named Dunkirque (Dunkirk) and the operation, named Dynamo, began on 27th May, just seventeen days after the Blitzkrieg had begun. On the 28th May, the French army began defending the area around Lille to stall the Germans and give the British a chance to get away. They held up for four days before the Germans punched their way through, but it had done the trick. By the 4th of June the evacuation was complete, so that most of the British force had escaped, along with many French soldiers.

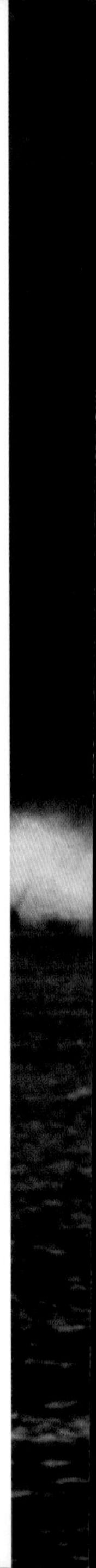

The port Dunkirk shrouded in smoke after fires had been started by German bombing

Over nine-hundred vessels had been used to evacuate 198,000 British and 140,000 French troops back to British shores. The majority of the rescue fleet had been non-military boats responding to the crisis and risking shellfire to stow as many soldiers as they could. Some craft made several round trips over the nine days of evacuation, which saved a third of a million combatants from death or incarceration. More importantly, it meant that the Allies still had an intact fighting force, albeit stationed on the wrong side of the English Channel.

So, the Germans had won the Battle of France in some style, but that was just one battle with many more to come. A little over four years later, many of those evacuees would return to French shores as part of the Normandy Landings and begin the process of pushing the Germans all the way back to Germany.

The evacuation of Dunkirque has taken its place in British folklore, because it was a classic example of people making the best out of a bad situation. The participation of so many civilians also demonstrated cohesion of spirit against the enemy and gave the British something to be positive about at a time when their future was by no means certain.

The ruins of Dunkirk after the fighting had ceased

Tanks Come of Age

The tank was first conceived by the British during World War I, as a means of crossing the battleground under machine gun fire to break the deadlock of trench warfare.

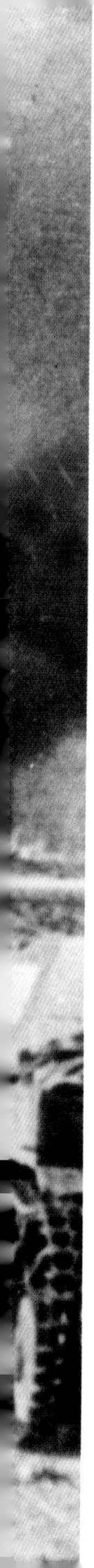

By the close of World War I the French had come up with the design that would become the standard format for tanks as we know them today. The Renault FT had a rotating gun turret mounted on an armoured chassis with the engine positioned at the rear and the driver positioned at the fore. This pattern set the standard that saw tanks evolve into efficient fighting machines during the interwar years.

The Germans developed a series of Panzer tank prototypes over the 1930s. They were considered to be better designed than most of the tanks of the Allies, in terms of reliability, manoeuvrability and weaponry, but it was the Blitzkrieg tactics that made them so much more effective in the field of battle, as it enabled the Germans to avoid one-to-one tank confrontations. The Germans were also the first to fully equip their tank corps with radio communications, which made a vast difference in terms of strategy. The Panzer III and Panzer IV were the models used in the early part of World War II. They were relatively small tanks and by the close of the war the Germans had introduced a medium tank in the form of the Panther and a large tank in the form of the Tiger. The Panther was a particularly effective weapon and set the benchmark for all post-war tanks.

Panzer units of the German Army pass through a blazing Russian village

The Russians prompted the Germans to improve their tanks, because they had a model called the T-34, which proved superior to the Panzers on the Eastern Front. Britain had various Cruiser and Infantry tanks, but also used American General and Sherman tanks. Sherman tanks were cheap to mass produce, which is what the USA did best, so there were plenty available even though they lacked sophistication and quality. Two or three Sherman tanks against a Panzer were always going to win, even though inferior in design. In the end this was a critical factor against the Germans, as they lacked the resources to manufacture enough of their tanks, partly because their quality standards were too high.

The Japanese had well designed tanks too, but they were not frequently used due to geography. In fact, they kept many of their tanks in reserve in case they had to defend their homelands, so they were never used. The Chi models of tank were the most advanced of the Japanese designs.

A US M4 Sherman tank

Turret crew of a 1st Royal Tank Regiment A9 Cruiser Mk I tank at Abbasia, Egypt

Aeroplanes Come of Age

The aeroplane was still in its infancy during the years of World War I. It began life as a reconnaissance vehicle, but its potential as a weapon was becoming evident as more reliable and faster models were being produced. By the close of the war, the aeroplane was beginning to evolve into particular classes of aircraft too, so that the concept of fighters and bombers had emerged.

During the interwar years the aeroplane continued to evolve rapidly. As engines developed to become more powerful relative to size, this meant that faster, stronger and heavier aeroplanes could be engineered. The aeroplane was no longer a flimsy, slow moving target, but a sleek, fast-moving war machine.

With increased speed, most aeroplanes became monoplanes to optimize their performance and manoeuvrability, and most adopted the standard format of fuselage with two flight wings to the fore and tail-plane to the rear. Other designs were all variations on the same theme even though they could be quite varied in detail.

Henschel HS 123 Dive Bomber. This single-seat biplane with swastika was originally used by the German Luftwaffe during the Spanish Civil War

Bombers needed to have large wing areas and a number of engines to provide sufficient payload, not just for bombs, but also for the fuel necessary for long-distance missions and the crews needed to fly, navigate and defend the aircraft. Fighters needed to be single-engined with relatively low wing area to make them fast and acrobatic in the air. They needed to carry sufficient fuel to escort bombers, but they had only a single pilot and machine guns.

There were intermediate aeroplanes too, in the form of fighter-bombers, which were somewhere between the two in terms of size, speed and payload. They were designed for medium range missions, where they could fly alone and make more precise bombing raids at low altitude. The Germans developed a fourth type of combat aeroplane, known as the dive-bomber.

Japanese seaplane wrecked during the battle of Makin, November 1943

German machine gunner in
a military aircraft, 1939

The idea was that the aircraft would dive towards its target and jettison its bombs forwards before levelling off. That way, it could hit the target with deadly precision.

A range of support aircraft were also developed for various purposes. There were cargo planes to transport supplies, equipment and personnel. There were also light aircraft for reconnaissance work and for covert field operations. A number of seaplanes were also developed to utilize flat-water for landing and taking off where runways were unavailable. Many fighters were also adapted for use on aircraft carriers, which were basically mobile runways and fuelling depots.

The wreckage of a German Heinkel bomber which crashed on the north-east coast of Britain after an encounter with RAF fighters

The Battle of Britain

Having conquered France and driven the British expeditionary force back across the English Channel, Hitler had designs on invading the British Isles, which he called Operation Sea Lion. In order to prepare for the planned invasion he knew that it was essential to first take on the RAF, so that the British would lack the air support necessary to defend their coastline against the offensive. So, the Luftwaffe was tasked with the job of destroying the British Air Force. The ensuing war for air superiority became known as the Battle of Britain.

As the Battle of Britain was primarily fought in the air, it meant that fighters were the key aircraft. The British had the Hurricane and the Spitfire at their disposal, while the Germans had the Messerschmitt Me109 and the twin-engined Messerschmitt Me110. In terms of hierarchy, relating to all-round performance, the Spitfire came first, followed by the Me109, then the Hurricane and the Me110. This gave the British the technical advantage, but they had fewer aircraft, so the odds were about even. Britain had just short of two thousand aeroplanes, while Germany had just over two and a half thousand.

A squadron of German Messerschmitt 110 fighter-bombers flies in formation

G

A Spitfire I, one of the first to be supplied to the RAF

19

Strategy, tactics and intelligence were therefore central to tipping the odds in favour of the British. Hugh Dowding had the position of Fighter Command at the start of the battle, on 10th July, 1940. He implemented very efficient ways of utilizing the resources available to him. In particular, he had small squadrons scattered across the country and an advanced radar system, which allowed pilots to be scrambled at a moment's notice to intercept enemy aircraft. By a process of attrition, the Luftwaffe was systematically depleted of its aircraft, until the battle was declared won by the British on the 31st October, 1940.

The British Prime Minister, Winston Churchill, was moved to say "Never before, in the field of human conflict, was so much owed, by so many, to so few." In winning the Battle of Britain, the RAF had caused Hitler to postpone Operation Sea Lion until the following year. By then, his concerns lay at the Eastern Front and Britain was left to lay its plans for an eventual counter offensive. In anticipation of a possible invasion, Churchill had also said "We shall fight on the beaches, we shall fight on the landing grounds, we shall fight in the fields and in the streets, we shall fight in the hills; we shall never surrender," but as it turned out the Battle of Britain had prevented that eventuality.

Volunteer American pilots during the Battle of Britain

Domestic War Effort

Fundamental to all successful war campaigns is logistics - organizing the manufacture of resources and the administration of their supply to where they are needed. When Britain realized that World War II was going to take a long time and rely heavily on effective logistical management, the government had to make some vital decisions and issue directives to the general population in order to involve the entire nation with the war effort.

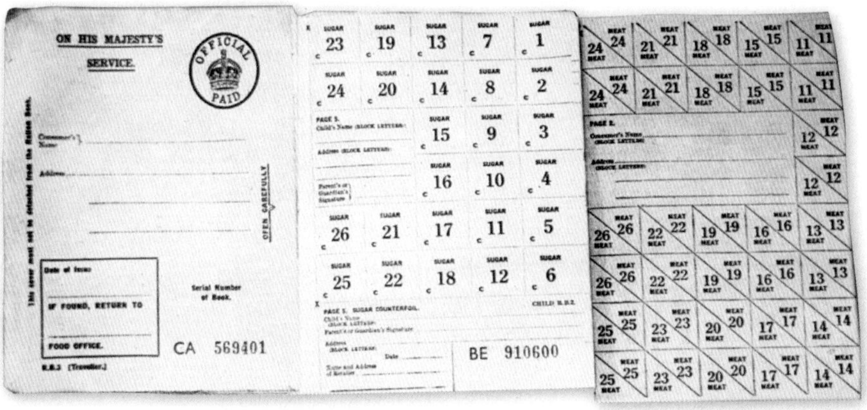

A close-up of a British ration book

Recruitment poster for the Women's Land Army

Hawker 'Hurricane' planes from no.111 squadron

Rationing was an important part of this objective as it meant that people were only too aware of the need to value and conserve basic resources, such as foodstuffs and domestic substances, such as washing powder and soap. This was partly because the forces needed to be supplied with basic necessities overseas, but it was also because many goods were imported and vessels were put to better use carrying cargoes of war equipment and munitions. In addition, German submarines were doing a very good job at preventing cargo ships from reaching the British Isles. As a way of supplementing their diets, the British people were encouraged to grow vegetables and rear livestock on any available plot of land, and to make the most of seasonal harvests of fruits and nuts.

Another area, where the general population were asked to assist, was in the provision of war materials - particularly iron and aluminium. Iron was used for making armour plating, gun barrels and other engineering components, such as nuts, bolts, rivets, and cogwheels. Aluminium was used in the manufacture of aircraft, because it was lightweight. Other metals included lead, for bullets, and copper and brass for shell casings.

Women working in a munitions factory, 1943

Civilians were also asked to contribute their time and effort into war related duties, such as the manufacture of machines and weapons. Many women volunteered to work in factories, so that they could play their part in the war effort while their husbands, brothers and fathers were away. Their children had often been evacuated to live in rural locations where they were less likely to be bombed.

Many young women helped the war effort by leaving towns and cities to work on farms as 'land girls'. As most farm labourers had been enlisted into the army, air force and navy, the replacement workforce was extremely valuable in ensuring that British farms kept up production of cereals, vegetables, meats, eggs and dairy produce. The land girls were largely responsible for providing the nation with the rations it needed to survive the war.

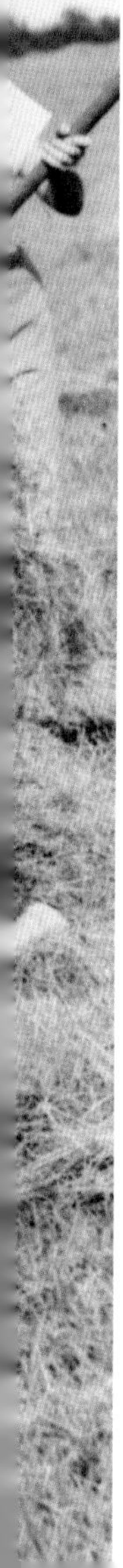

Members of the Women's Land Army gather the late harvest on a farm in Llangwm, Wales

Two Wehrmacht soldiers are holding a Swastika flag to protect against friendly fire during Operation Barbarossa

Operation Barbarossa

Following the German invasion of Poland in 1939, Hitler had agreed a pact of non-aggression with Russia in August of that year. At the time it suited Hitler to pretend that he had no interest in invading Russia, so that he could concentrate his resources in Western Europe. By the close of 1940 Hitler decided that he only needed an occupying force in the west, so he made plans to break his pact with Russia and head eastward. In the spring of 1941 he deployed a huge fighting force along the Eastern Front and launched their offensive, named Operation Barbarossa, on June 22nd.

At first the German assault was a success, as it had been on the Western Front. The Blitzkrieg tactics worked well and the Germans made rapid territorial gains. Hitler was delighted with progress and had every confidence that Moscow would be taken, so that Russia would become part of the Third Reich.

A soldier is guarding a village under the snow

Russian soldiers in the snow during winter
1941- 1942 on the Russian Front

However, things began to go wrong as winter closed in on the Germans. Muddy ground made it difficult for the frontline to move forward and it made the supply chain inefficient. In addition, the troops were ill-equipped to operate in the wet, cold conditions. When the Russian winter set in properly it was so cold that engines wouldn't start and soldiers were suffering from frostbite. The mighty German army had been halted by the Russian climate.

In addition, the Russian population was so large that Stalin had an almost endless supply of new troops. They died in vast numbers, but were replaced in equally vast numbers. Being used to their own climate, the Russians were also far better equipped, both physically and mentally, to cope with the conditions.

By December 1941 the Germans were only a matter of miles from Moscow, when Stalin gave the order for the Russian counter-offensive on December 5th.

The Germans were unable to defend their positions and were pushed into a retreat. By mid-December the weather was so cold that the Luftwaffe were unable to assist, because their aeroplanes were rendered inoperative by the sub-zero temperatures. Operation Barbarossa had turned from success to failure as the Germans were pushed ever farther west. Until weather conditions improved in 1942 there was little they could do to try turn matters back in their favour.

On December 5th, 1941, Stalin gave the order for the Russian counter-offensive during the Battle of Moscow

The Blitz

About halfway through the Battle of Britain, on September 7th 1940, the Germans began a strategic bombing campaign of British cities. It became known as the Blitz, not to be confused with the Blitzkrieg and would last for over eight months. The initial incentive for the bombing campaign was to strike at factories dedicated to the manufacture of aircraft, munitions and other equipment. Ports were also targeted to disrupt supply lines. However, bombing was not an accurate science in those days, especially under cover of darkness, so the majority of bombs missed their intended targets and randomly hit residential areas, killing many civilians.

The main cities bombed were London, Birmingham, Bristol, Plymouth, Southampton and Portsmouth. London suffered more bombing raids than the others combined, so sheltering became a matter of routine. In fact there was an average of around one raid every three or four days, so it was better to be safe than sorry. London lost more than a million homes and over forty thousand people lost their lives. Things were so dangerous that children had to be evacuated to live with families in rural locations for the duration.

Devastated buildings around St Paul's Cathedral, London, after an air raid during the Blitz

Firemen at work on fires, the result of bombs dropped by the Germans, near St Paul's Cathedral, London

TO LET

Despite the death and carnage visited on their city, Londoners displayed a behavioural cohesion known as the Blitz spirit, which saw people helping one another to cope with the practical problems and the emotional trauma experienced by so many.

Due to the inaccuracy of bombing, it was a matter of hit or miss as to whether strategic targets received bomb damage. Some raids were successful in halting British progress, but never for sustained periods of time. They also became self-defeating as the Blitz only prompted the British to mount retaliatory raids over Germany, so that their own wartime industries were disrupted. This tit-for-tat bombing continued as the war continued, but civilian deaths became an ethical issue. For one thing, the killing of children, women and the elderly seemed entirely unnecessary.

From the British point of view, there was also the notion that many of the German civilian population were not followers of the Nazi ideology, and were therefore innocent victims. Following the war, those who commanded and took part in bombing raids were not properly celebrated and recognized for their contribution to the war effort. This was because of an undercurrent of shame that the bombing of civilian areas had become a component of war. It didn't sit well with the idea that war should be conducted in an honourable way.

Londoners sheltering in an Underground station during an air raid

North Africa Campaign

The North Africa Campaign began when the British decided it would be strategically useful to control the Mediterranean Sea, with a view to launching a counter-offensive against the European Axis from the south. At the time, the region was occupied by Italian forces.

Below; Two soldiers belonging to the Commonwealth and Allied forces aim at a German soldier surrendering atop his tank 25 October 1942 as a sandstorm clouds the battlefield at El Alamein

Below; Tommies of the British forces toil in the heat of the midday sun, in the shadow of the Egyptian pyramids

The Italians were no match for the British and were pushed into retreat, but Hitler responded by deploying German forces under the command of Erwin Rommel and the complexion of the campaign changed very quickly. There was now parity between the Allied and Axis forces, which resulted in a protracted series of battles, causing the frontline to sweep back and forth as offensives and counter-offensives were launched.

The campaign began in June 1940 and would drag out until May of 1943. The Second Battle of El Alamein (Oct-Nov 1942) is recognized as a seminal moment in World War II, because it was the first time the Allies had achieved a decisive victory against the Axis. Responding to news of the German defeat, Winston Churchill commented in a speech "Now this is not the end. It is not even the beginning of the end. But it is, perhaps, the end of the beginning". He wanted to accentuate the positive outcome, but he also wanted to make it clear that the war was a long way from being won. Following the eventual Allied victory, he commented that the battle had indeed been a turning point in the war as, from that point onwards, the Germans were on the back foot. Momentum had shifted in the Allies' favour.

British tanks proceeding along the waterfront in Benghazi as the 8th Army advance in Libya

The North Africa Campaign was characterized by the desert terrain, typical of the coastline of the southern Mediterranean. This meant that there was no cover, either from the elements or from enemy fire. Tanks, Howitzers and field guns played a central role in the theatre of battle, but the most critical element was one of logistics. As one side advanced, its supply lines became progressively stretched over barren terrain, making it harder and harder to keep the front moving.

At the same time, this meant that the supply lines of the opposing force were shortened, making it easier to reach the frontline. As a result, the battle front oscillated west-east/east-west a number of times, until attrition of the German reserves finally allowed the Allies to get the upper hand. The Axis was ultimately forced out of North Africa because sufficient reserves were not made available by Hitler, as he had more pressing concerns elsewhere.

The first British tank enters Tripoli, Libya with soldiers and a piper aboard the Valentine tank

Scottish Cameron Highlander and Indian troops marching past pyramids, part of Allied defence preparations against Italian attack

The American destroyer USS Shaw explodes during the Japanese attack on Pearl Harbor, 1941

Attack on Pearl Harbor

Late in 1941, the Japanese had plans to invade the southern reaches of Southeast Asia, including the northern coast of Australia. The indefatigable progress of the Nippon army had the Australians deeply fearful and the Americans were amassing a large fleet in the Pacific, in anticipation of their entry into the war. The Japanese were aware of the US military build-up and decided to force the situation in order to prevent the Americans from halting their empire building.

As the Japanese had not yet declared war on the USA they had a trick up their sleeve – the element of surprise. On the morning of December 7th, they launched an all-out offensive against the US military base at Pearl Harbor, Hawaii. The majority of the US fleet was moored-up in the harbour, so it was like shooting fish in a barrel.

USA warships on fire in Pearl Harbor, Oahu Island after a surprise attack by the Japanese

The Japanese used more than 350 aircraft and a number of mini-submarines to wreak havoc on the Americans before they knew what was happening.

Many important US vessels were destroyed and sunk during the attack, leaving the American fleet seriously depleted. However, the Japanese had failed to destroy many of the essential dock facilities, which meant that recovery was reasonably rapid. Also, both of the US aircraft carriers and their escort convoys happened to be away from port at the time of the attack, so the core of the US fleet remained intact.

In effect, the Japanese had awakened a sleeping giant by attacking Pearl Harbor in the way they did, without declaring war. While the Japanese celebrated what they saw as a cunning victory,the Allies saw the assault as an underhand ambush.

The USS California on fire in Pearl Harbor

Troops salvage the wreckage following the attack on Pearl Harbor

New York World-Telegram

7TH SPORTS
LATEST RACING
Results on Page 26.
PRICE THREE CENTS

Local Forecast: Light rains tonight, somewhat higher temperatures than last night; tomorrow cloudy followed by clearing, cooler than today.

VOL. 74.—NO. 135.—IN TWO SECTIONS—SECTION ONE NEW YORK, MONDAY, DECEMBER 8, 1941.

1500 DEAD IN HAWAII

Congress Votes War on Japan; Manila Bases Bombed Again

Tally in Senate Is 82 to 0, In House 388 to 1, with Miss Rankin Sole Objector

BULLETIN.

By the United Press.

WASHINGTON, Dec. 8.—President Roosevelt at 4:10 p. m. today signed the joint Congressional resolution declaring existence of a state of war with the Japanese Empire.

By LYLE C. WILSON.

WASHINGTON, Dec. 8.—Congress today proclaimed existence of a state of war between the United States and the Japanese Empire 33 minutes after President Roosevelt stood before a joint session to ask such action and pledge that we will triumph—"so help us, God."

Democracy was proving its right to a place in the sun with a split-second shiftover from peace to all-out war.

The Senate acted first, adopting the resolution by a unanimous roll call vote of 82 to 0, within 21 minutes after the President had concluded his address, amid tumultuous cheering of both houses.

The House vote was 388 to 1.

The lone dissenting vote was cast by Representative Rankin (R., Mont.). It was she who in the small hours of April 6, 1917, faltered, wept and finally voted no against a similar resolution aimed at Germany.

A chorus of hisses and boos greeted her vote.

100 to 200 Soldiers Killed in Japanese Raid On Luzon in Philippines

By the United Press.

WASHINGTON, Dec. 8. — Casualties on the Hawaiian island of Oahu in yesterday's Japanese air attack will amount to about 3000, including about 1500 fatalities, the White House announced today.

The White House confirmed the loss in Pearl Harbor of "one old battleship" and a destroyer, which was blown up.

Several other American ships were damaged and a large number of army and navy airplanes on Hawaiian fields were put out of commission, the White House disclosed.

The White House statement said:

"American operations against the Japanese attacking force in the neighborhood of the Hawaiian Islands are still continuing. A number of Japanese planes and submarines have been destroyed.

"The damage caused to our forces in Oahu in yesterday's attack appears more serious than at first believed.

"In Pearl Harbor itself one old battleship has capsized and several other ships have been seriously damaged.

"One destroyer was blown up. Several other small ships were seriously hurt. Army and navy fields were bombed with the resulting destruction of several hangars. A large number of planes were put out of commission.

"Guam, Wake and Midway Islands and Hong Kong have been attacked. Details of these attacks are lacking.

"Two hundred marines—all that remain in China—have been interned by the Japanese near Tientsin.

"The total number of casualties on the island of Oahu are not yet definitely known but, in all probability, will mount to about 3000. Nearly half of these are fatalities, the others being wounded.

Roosevelt's War Message To Congress

Navy Enlistment Office Swamped by Volunteers

Number Quitting Jobs to Join Is Double That of Last War

Britain Declares War on Japan

Becomes Ally of U. S., China and Thailand

The Weather

All Draft Quotas To Be Increased

Japanese Claim Naval Supremacy

Four Battleships, a Carrier, Six Cruisers Reported Hit

Churchill Tells World of War Aim

Suicide Leaves Note

World-Telegram Index

Japanese Planes Set Big Fires in Manila

Gasoline Dumps Are Believed Hit—Antiaircraft Guns Fire

The front page of the 'New York World Telegram'

In 1937 the Japanese had behaved in a similar way by opening hostilities against China without declaring war. In repeating this unsporting approach, the Japanese had done themselves no favours as it revealed an underlying disrespect for other nations and fuelled Allied determination to put them in their place.

Once the USA was committed to the war, it wanted revenge for Pearl Harbor, so the Japanese had a determined foe on their tail. It took some time for the Americans to replenish their fleet and develop the right strategy for dealing with ensconced Japanese occupying forces, but eventually they were systematically flushing the enemy from one island after the next and forcing the Japanese to constrict their ambitions of empire.

PERRAUD

Vichy France

Following the Fall of France in the Summer of 1940, the French government felt compromised and reached a peace agreement with Germany in order to save France from being portioned out between the Axis powers. In effect, France became a state of the Third Reich, known as Vichy France. The northern region remained occupied by German forces to defend against possible invasion from across the English Channel, while the southern region was the 'free zone' and maintained its sovereignty.

General Charles de Gaulle had fled to exile in London, from where he rallied support against German occupation of France. He also maintained political opposition towards Marshall Philippe Pétain who had assumed leadership of the regime in collusion with the Germans. Many of those still living in France, who opposed Pétain and the Germans, joined the French resistance movement, named the Maquis. Many of the rest of the population did their best to support and assist the Maquis in their covert operations, by hiding weapons and protecting people when they could.

There was also a Europe-wide resistance network to help enemies of the Axis travel through occupied Europe without being captured. This included

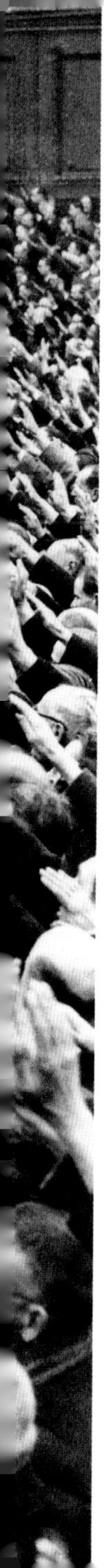

Hitler salute at Vichy In France

downed airmen, escaped prisoners, special agents, covert operatives, Jews and fellow resistance personnel.

Algeria, in North Africa, was a French colony when Germany conquered France, so it became part of Vichy France, providing the Axis with control of Algeria in 1940. However, the Vichy army offered only half-hearted resistance against the Allies when they decided to invade Algiers in November 1942, because many were reluctantly fighting for the Axis. As a result, Operation Torch was a success and gave the Allies a solid foothold on the southern Mediterranean coast. This contributed to the British success at El Alamein, because it improved supply lines at a critical juncture.

By chance, the commander in chief of the French Navy, Admiral François Darlan, had travelled to Angiers the day before the invasion and was captured. He turned against the Vichy government by deciding to express allegiance with the Allies. As a result, Hitler sent reinforcements to North Africa and ordered the occupation of Vichy France by German and Italian troops to protect the Mediterranean coast of France. However, in North Africa the tables were already turning in favour of the Allies, whose next move would be to make preparations for invading Italy.

American troops wade ashore near Oran, Algeria, during Operation Torch, November 1942

Henri Philippe Petain (left), French general and later Chief of State
of Vichy France

War in the Atlantic

As World War II progressed, Britain and its allies relied ever more heavily on goods and equipment being shipped from the Americas across the Atlantic Ocean. As a result, the Atlantic became a hunting ground for German submarines, which were known as U-boats. As any large vessels were quite likely to be carrying goods essential for the Allied war effort, in one way or another, the U-boats targeted indiscriminately with their torpedoes.

This meant that ships were theoretically safer travelling in convoy, with armed escorts. However, it was a double-edged sword, as groups of ships made much easier targets for the U-boats. They were more likely to make a hit and they also had the chance to sink a number of boats in a single raid.

German sailors crouch down by the U-boat's conning tower as they manoeuvre against an attack by American B-25 Mitchell and B-24 Liberator bombers, 1944

A German U-boat, which was captured in the Atlantic

The U-boats also found easy pickings along the American coast. As the Americans were not initially involved directly in the war, they had a rather naïve understanding of the U-boat threat. In particular, they made no effort to blackout their cities, which meant that cargo vessels were nicely silhouetted against the lights at night, making them extremely easy targets for the submarines. They just had to sit in wait and fire torpedoes at will.

However, the Germans didn't have it all their own way. By now sonar had been invented, which enabled warships to detect submarines whilst submerged. Just as radar used reflecting radio waves, so sonar used reflecting sound waves. When sound waves arrived back at the ship, it was possible to approximate the distance, the depth and the direction of travel of the submarine.

Depth charges would then be used to bombard the area, in the hope that the shock waves would crack the hull of the U-boat. The development of sonar meant that U-boats had to quickly escape after making their attacks to avoid being caught in a net of underwater explosions.

Sometimes, cornered U-boats would pretend to be destroyed by sinking to the seabed and jettisoning oil and cargo as flotsam to create the right impression. They would then sit for hours in total silence until the enemy decided to move off.

Another interesting development came in the form of dazzle and cryptic camouflage of warships. By painting vessels with inventive patterns and shades it was possible to create optical illusions from a distant viewpoint. The idea was that U-boat commanders would be fooled by what they saw through their periscopes. In some cases camouflage would render vessels invisible, while in other instances ships could be made to look back-to-front or to look like more than one boat in convoy. By confusing the eyes, it was hoped that torpedo attacks might be less likely, either for fear of counter attack or wasting torpedoes.

Russian Navy firing depth charge at German U-boat

U-boats stranded on the south coast of England after surrender

Sieges of Leningrad and Stalingrad

During Operation Barbarossa the German Army surrounded the Russian city of Leningrad. The occupants of the city put up a fierce resistance, so the Germans besieged Leningrad in September 1941. The Germans hadn't bargained on the Russians being so tenacious in their determination to prevent the Germans from taking the city and the siege lasted for almost 900 days, finally ending in Jan 1944 when the Eastern Front was pushed back towards Germany by the Soviet Army.

By the end of the Siege of Leningrad the city lay in ruins, but had never been taken by the Germans because the Russians had established a heavily fortified zone, which formed an impenetrable nucleus. As well as the material cost, the human cost was enormous, with around 1.5 million Russian soldiers and civilians dead.

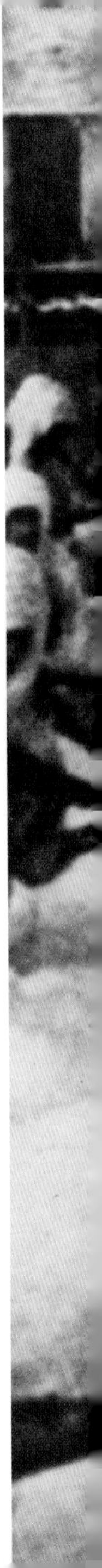

Russian army in snow camouflage advances against the Germans, 1944

Due to injury, the insanitary conditions and starvation, a further 2.5 million were suffering from illness and disease, but victory belonged to the Soviets.

Leningrad (now St. Petersburg) lies on the coast of the Baltic Sea, to the north of Russia's western border and was strategically desirable to the Germans as a port. Stalingrad (now Volgograd) lies to the south-west of Russia and was strategically desirable because of its industrial facilities and its proximity to the Baku and Maikop oil fields, needed for fuel and lubricants.

The Germans launched an extension to Operation Barbarossa in June 1942, named Operation Braunschweig, with the intention of occupying the Caucuses region. In August they reached Stalingrad and the Germans laid siege.

This siege was relatively short-lived, lasting for just over six months, but it was no less bloody than the Siege of Leningrad, with hundreds of thousands killed or injured, on both sides.

German machine gunner on the Russian Front, 1943

The Germans came close to defeating the Russians, but the Soviet army managed to surround the enemy while they were focused on taking the city. The successful Soviet offensive was named Operation Uranus. The Germans wanted to make a thrusting assault westward to escape the encirclement, but Hitler ordered the army to stay and fight, believing they could still succeed if the Luftwaffe provided an airborne supply line. He was wrong, as a second Russian winter and heavy anti-aircraft fire prevented the Luftwaffe from reaching the beleaguered German army.

The pocket of territory held by the Germans was gradually constricted by the persistent Soviet pressure, until the remaining forces surrendered in February 1943, against Hitler's wishes.

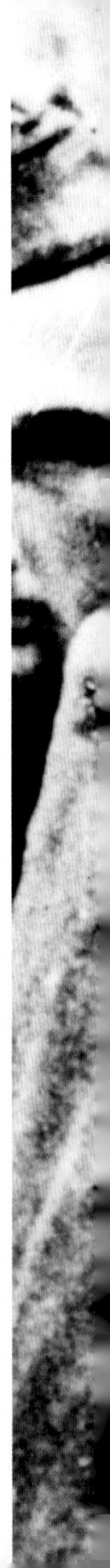

German prisoners with soldiers from other Axis satellite countries, huddle against the sharp winds of the Russian winter, after the defeat of the German Army at Stalingrad, February 1943

Burma Campaign

During the Japanese advance of World War II, the Japanese troops cultivated quite a reputation for their hardiness in the field. In the jungles of Burma, the Allied forces found life very hard going and were driven out by the Japanese, who coped far better with the tropical conditions and therefore had higher morale and better vigour. The Allies were beset with illness, disease, pestilence and fatigue, because they simply didn't know how to look after themselves in the jungle environment. Meanwhile, the Japanese made the most of the natural resources available, keeping themselves well fed, comfortable and free from ailments.

Having been forced to retreat from Burma in early 1942, the Allies then spent two years trying to mount counter-offensives, but they just couldn't compete with the Japanese prowess at jungle warfare.

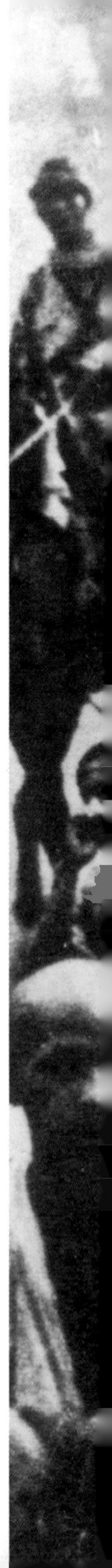

Burmese locals show little interest in the arrival of the Japanese occupying forces in their village, 1942

In addition, the Allies learnt to fear the Japanese on a one-to-one basis, because they were known to charge at the enemy with a frightening battle cry and an apparent disregard for their own safety. This was because the Japanese wanted to die an honourable death in devotion to their emperor, so they were not afraid to commit themselves. After a while though, the Allies realized that the Japanese were quite frenzied and unfocused in this behaviour, so they were quite easy to shoot dead while they charged because they had no strategy.

In early 1944 the Japanese made a tactical error. They made a failed attempt to invade India, which left them depleted of personnel and resources. This marked the perfect opportunity for the Allies to finally launch a successful offensive and push the Japanese back out of Burma.

A similar pattern occurred elsewhere. The Japanese had invaded the entirety of South-east Asia, but they stretched themselves too far and allowed the momentum to shift in favour of the Allies. They found themselves defending their new empire with ever decreasing manpower and supplies, so retreat to a smaller area of territory to defend was an inevitable conclusion. This process was accelerated by the involvement of the USA, as it poured in all it could to the Allied war effort and developed strategies to flush the Japanese out of the many occupied islands in the region.

Lord Louis Mountbatten, British Admiral (Commander-in-chief of the Allied forces of Southeast Asia) on the Front of Burma, March 1944

Japanese troops crossing the Salween River to land at Martaban, during the fall of Rangoon

B

Chinese tank crew on their American-made M-5 light tank, Hukawng Valley, Burma, April 1944

Battle of Midway

In June, 1942, the Americans found the Japanese fleet, six months after the Attack on Pearl Harbor, and exacted their revenge. The Japanese had been preparing to attack the Americans at Midway Island, which lies in the North Pacific Ocean roughly halfway between North America and Asia, as its name alludes.

The US force knew the Japanese were somewhere in the area, so they were on the lookout. On the morning of the 4th, a group of US Devastator torpedo bombers located the Japanese and engaged. Most were shot down by the Japanese, but they failed to notice an approaching squadron of thirty-three Dauntless dive-bombers dispatched from the USS Enterprise aircraft carrier, and a second squadron of seventeen Dauntless dive-bombers from USS Yorktown.

Smoking hulk of the Japanese heavy cruiser Mikuma, which was destroyed during the decisive Battle of Midway

American aircraft Douglas Dauntless dive-bombers used during the Battle of Midway against Japanese in the Pacific War

The Japanese defending squadron of Zero fighters had already been scrambled against the Devastators, so they had used their ammunition and were also flying at sea level. When the dive-bombers attacked from above there was nothing the Japanese could do to prevent the US bombs from striking their vessels. Four aircraft carriers were lost to the Americans, along with hundreds of aircraft, and the Japanese no longer had a functioning fleet.

The Japanese had gone to Midway with the intention of finishing off the US fleet but been trounced instead. The Americans got lucky on the 4th June, allowing them to tackle the Japanese fleet virtually untouched, due to fortuitous timing. Thus, the USA had its revenge for Pearl Harbor and turned the war in its favour with one fell-swoop.

The Americans were now able to navigate the war zone with relative impunity, as the Japanese could only dispatch aeroplanes from island bases over a limited flight range. The US then set about systematically taking the islands with airstrips, so that the Japanese were progressively restricted in their military movements and in a perpetual state of defence and retreat. In a maritime theatre of war, having naval supremacy meant victory was inevitable for the US, although it would take another three years of ferocious fighting to achieve, such was the Japanese will.

Smoke from anti-aircraft guns fills the sky as aircraft carrier USS Yorktown is hit by a Japanese torpedo during the Battle of Midway

Pilots for the American Navy Torpedo bomber squadron prior to the Battle of Midway, in which all but one would be killed.

Women at War

World War II marked a significant gender shift in society. Women made a significant contribution to the war effort in a number of direct and indirect ways. Civilian women worked the land and worked in factories to ensure that rations and resources were made available in large enough quantities to satisfy the basic human needs of the population. Many other women were trained to manufacture munitions, equipment and machines needed in the theatre of battle.

They became highly skilled engineers and technicians, and were often better than their male counterparts because they had a finesse and mindset better suited to the exacting work. By taking on these traditionally male roles, they freed up the men to join the forces, where they could be more useful.

An auxiliary of the US Army

That didn't mean though, that women were not enlisted into the forces. There were many supporting roles within the army, navy and air force that women were able to perform. In fact, they had their own equivalent sections within the forces. In the navy they belonged to the Women's Royal Naval Service (WRNS) otherwise known as the 'Wrens'.

In the air force they belonged to the Women's Royal Air Force (WRAF) and were known as 'Wrafs'. In the army, they belonged to the Women's Royal Army Corps (WRAC) and were called 'Wracs'. In these sections they performed all kinds of back-up duties, such as operating supply lines, transporting personnel and equipment, repairs, maintenance and administration.

Basically, they did any jobs that weren't considered to place them in situations of high risk at the frontline. That didn't mean they were safe, however, as many military women fell victim to bombing raids.

Women also played an important role in the Royal Army Medical Corps (RAMC) which performed essential work tending the sick and injured in warzones. There was even a Royal Army Dental Corps (RADC) which became officially titled in 1946 in recognition of its value during World War II.

Armed service recruiting poster, 1942

E
E

In the WRAF there was a unit called the Air Transport Auxiliary (ATA). This was home to a number of female wartime pilots, whose job it was to deliver and collect military aircraft, so that fighter and bomber squadrons had the serviceable aeroplanes they needed to conduct their missions.

A few women were also involved with the entertainment of troops, as comediennes, singers, dancers and members of musical troupes. Some were music hall celebrities, such as Gracie Fields and Vera Lynn, who would perform with forces orchestras, both in Britain and overseas.

Iconic patriotic poster by J. Howard Miller featuring woman factory worker in bandana rolling up her sleeve & flexing her arm muscles

Three female Wren Air mechanics at a dive bomber station

Indian servicewomen in their traditional saris – they are members of the Women's Royal Naval Service, Women's Auxiliary Army Corps, and the Auxiliary Territorial Service

The Holocaust

It is fair to say that the Nazis had an obsessive hatred for the Jewish race, which became the focal point of their ideology. Historically, anti-Semitism was rooted in the fact that Jews were allowed to lend money for profit, which was a practice frowned upon by other religions. In addition, the Jews had been uprooted from their traditional home, which meant that they had to live itinerant lives, travelling around Europe to make their living. They inadvertently cultivated a stereotypical image, as outsiders with strange ways and questionable ethics, who kept themselves to themselves and found advantage in other people's misfortune.

As it is always easier to blame others when the chips are down, Hitler and his supporters found it convenient to target the Jews as responsible for the German hyper-inflation during the Great Depression. While the German population struggled to avoid destitution, some Jews seemed to be relatively comfortable, because they existed within a sub-culture.

Child survivors of Auschwitz show their tattooed arms, Poland, February 1945

A large group of Jews, escorted by soldiers of the SS, are taken to a concentration camp before the crowds at the roadside

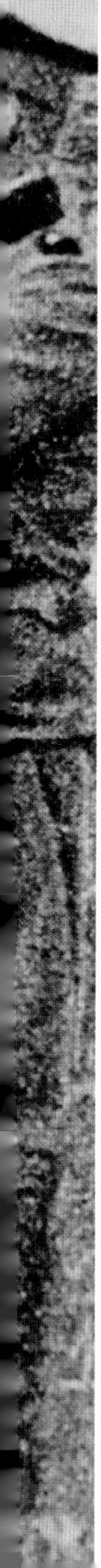

It didn't take much imagination for the Nazis to falsely claim that the Jews had a hand in the fiscal demise of Germany, and it took even less imagination for the general population to believe the Nazis. The power of simple suggestion is potent among people who cannot comprehend the complexity of truth.

The Nazis began their persecution of the Jews by ghettoizing them, to keep them all in one place and out of social circulation. They then began shipping them to remote locations and systematically shooting them, but their scale of ambition was such that they could not process sufficient numbers to keep up with the supply of Jews arriving from all over occupied Europe. This prompted the Nazis to devise more efficient ways of killing Jews and disposing of their remains.

In early 1942, Auschwitz, one of the most notorious death camps, began the terrible practice of gassing and burning Jews en masse. Any Jews considered useful were housed in a concentration camp and put to labour, while those of no value to the war effort were murdered and incinerated next door. A number of similar camps were constructed to cater for Nazi demand in other regions.

Nazi leader and war criminal Adolf Eichmann (2nd right) smiling while German officers cut a Jewish prisoner's hair

The Nazis continued with this ethnic cleansing until the Allies encountered the camps as they advanced across Europe towards Germany. Needless to say, the discovery that the Nazis were capable of such inhumanity to man only fuelled the Allied determination to thoroughly stamp them out of history.

Even to this day, what the Nazis did was so shocking and unspeakable that some people find it hard to believe that it happened. Were it not for the evidence and the witnesses it would indeed be difficult to accept that humans are capable of such horrific crimes against their own species.
The way the Nazis engineered the Holocaust was by dehumanizing the Jews to make it easier to commit their wrongs. By removing their clothes and possessions, and shaving their heads, the Nazis removed individuality and personality in the Jews, so that they became a uniform population of clones.

The gates of the Nazi concentration camp at Auschwitz, Poland; the sign above them reads 'Arbeit Macht Frei' - 'Work Makes You Free'

MACHT FREI

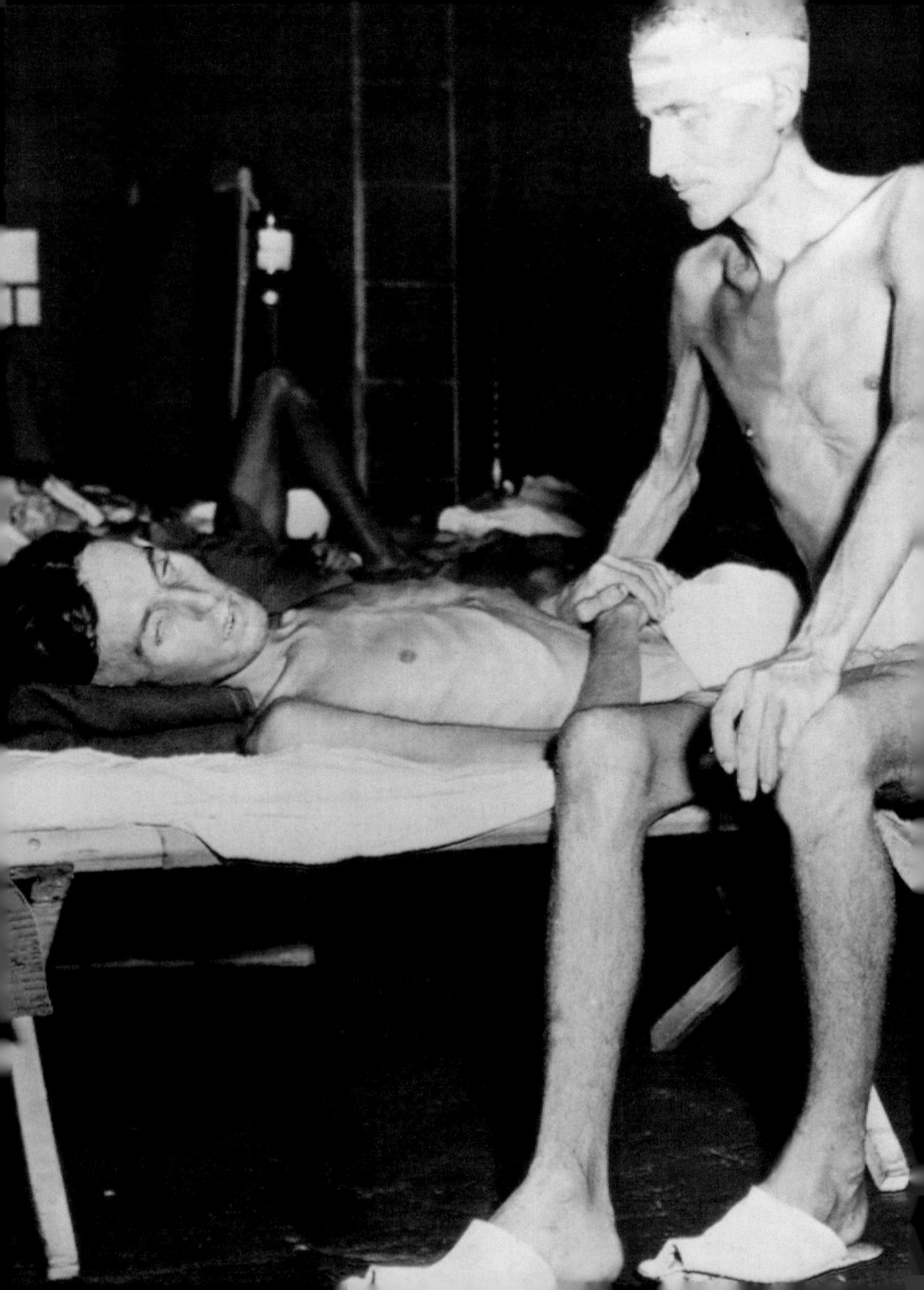

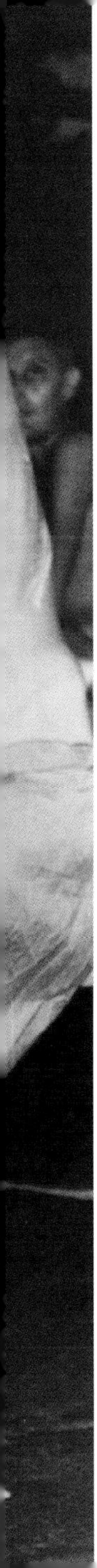

Japanese POWs

While the Nazis' treatment of Jews was despicable, they were relatively less cruel to their POWs in general, although torture and execution were commonplace among prisoners who were suspected of spying against the Third Reich.

The Japanese were the ones who treated their POWs with contempt, because they had the overriding view that all other races were inferior to them. Also, the very idea of surrender or being caught by the enemy went against the Japanese ethos, so those who allowed themselves to become POWs were to be regarded as weak and unworthy of respect.

The Japanese would nearly always opt for an honourable death, rather than fall prisoner, and this ideal influenced the way they treated those who chose to remain alive by becoming captive.

Two liberated British POWs from a Japanese prison camp in 1945

British soldiers taken prisoner by the Japanese in Singapore, 1942

The Bataan Death March is one of the most notorious examples of the Japanese treatment of POWs. On April 9th 1942 many US and Filipino prisoners were forced to begin an eighty mile march to the prison camp in which they were to be held, following their capture after the Battle of Bataan.

The prisoners were beaten and given insufficient medical care, food and rest, so many died from their injuries, exhaustion and disease along the way. Some were murdered when their condition prevented them from continuing with the journey. There were also a number of death marches from Sandakan to Ranau, in Borneo, where similar treatment of prisoners was standard practice by the Japanese.

For those who survived the death marches, there was worse to come at the hands of those who ran the prison camps. Many were cruelly tortured and starved to death or executed by sword or gun for no particular reason than the amusement of the Japanese guards and officers, who found their duties tedious and viewed the prisoners as sub-human.

Japanese soldiers march prisoners of war, with arms raised, across the Bataan peninsula in what became known as the Bataan Death March, Luzon, Philippines

In addition to their POW camps, the Japanese also had many internment camps for civilian prisoners, who were also kept in appalling conditions and given woeful treatment.

Many of these civilian prisoners were European colonialists who failed to escape the advancing Japanese. By and large, the native populations of invaded territories were allowed to continue their lives in freedom, although under Japanese occupation, so that they contributed to the war effort. Many indigenous peoples enjoyed a new found liberation from servitude when the Japanese arrived, because their colonial bosses had either fled or been incarcerated. This prompted a general shift towards political independence across the region following the war.

Survivors of the Dachau concentration camp at the arrival of the VIIth American army

Italy Campaign

Winston Churchill described Italy as the soft underbelly of Nazi occupied Europe. The Italians were not renowned for their fighting ability, having been easily beaten back by the Allies in North Africa. Hitler was aware that the Mediterranean coast presented a point of vulnerability, but by 1943 he was occupied with developments on the Eastern Front, and he wasn't entirely sure where the Allies might try their luck at a counter-offensive. France offered the most practical landing points, so Axis forces had been stationed along the French coast in anticipation of defensive action.

The Allies went for Italy, precisely because it seemed an unlikely strategic choice and was therefore not defended as well as it might have been. On the 10th July, the Allies mounted an assault of the island of Sicily, to give them a foothold on Italian soil, from where they could launch their offensive of mainland Italy.

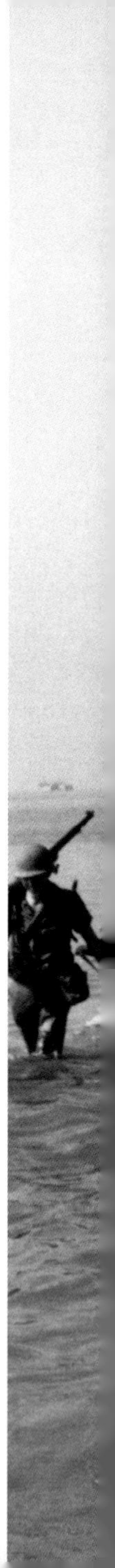

American troops wading ashore from a landing craft during the World War II Allied invasion of Italy

220
220

9

By the time the Allies were ready for the second phase they had, of course, lost any element of surprise and Hitler had deployed German forces to counter the threat, but the Allied occupation of Sicily was key, as it provided a base for naval, army and air forces. This meant that the Allies could attack with sufficient resources to be certain of making successful landings on the Italian coast.

The invasion properly began on 3rd September, with British troops landing on the 'toe' of the Italian peninsula. This was called Operation Baytown. Realizing that the Allies meant business, the Italian government surrendered on 8th September, but the Germans intended to fight. The next day, two Allied invasion forces launched assaults in different regions.

Operation Slapstick hit Taranto, in the 'arch of the foot' of the Italian Peninsula. The combatants met with little resistance, as the Germans were expecting an invasion attempt of the west coast. Meanwhile, Operation Avalanche struck the beaches of Salerno, on the 'shin' of the Italian peninsula. Here, the Germans put up fierce resistance and it took quite a battle for the Allies to establish a beachhead.

A group of British soldiers put their shoulders to the side of a stationary truck during the Allied landing in southern Italy.

Italian soldiers surrendering
after the landing of Allied
forces in Sicily

Mussolini's Mistakes

Benito Mussolini rose to power in Italy in 1926, when he seized power as the leader of a fascist regime, in imitation of Adolf Hitler. In 1930 he named himself as Il Duce. Just as Hitler had seduced the Germans with the idea of the Third Reich becoming a new German empire, so Mussolini sold the idea of the 'New Roman Empire' in allusion to the illustrious past of his race.

Things went well for Mussolini until World War II revealed his incompetence as a military tactician, which led the Italian population to turn against him. One major setback was Italy's defeat in North Africa, alongside the Germans, which resulted in the loss of Italian colonial interests. When Operation Barbarossa began on the Eastern Front, Mussolini sent an Italian corps to contribute to the Axis war effort, even though Hitler had not expected the Italians to take part.

French troops disembark from ships to occupy the Island of Elba, 1944.

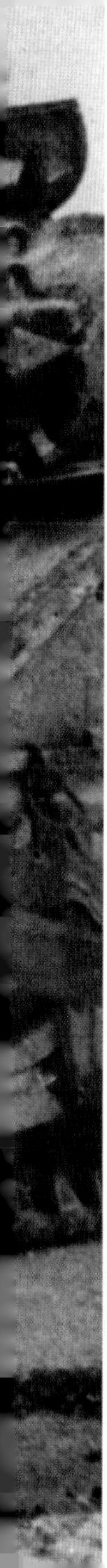

Mussolini clearly wanted to curry favour with Hitler and have the opportunity to save face by showing that the Italians were a fighting force equal to the Germans. When the tables turned in favour of the Russians, the Italian people were none too impressed by Mussolini's pandering at the expense of many lives.

Then, when the Allies invaded Sicily on 10th July, it was the final straw. The Italian industrial infrastructure and home front had taken a battering from Allied bombing, so the population had low morale. Mussolini had tried and failed to persuade Hitler to make peace with the Russians, so that Axis forces could be diverted to Italy to prevent an Allied invasion. Most of the Sicilians actually welcomed the arrival of the Allies and the Italian army was on the point of collapse.

On the night of 25th of July, Mussolini was arrested by the Italian military police. The Fascist Grand Council had decided to oust him from power and he was imprisoned. When Hitler learnt of Mussolini's arrest he launched plans for Germany to take control of Italy by arresting the entire government and royal family. The plan was to reinstate Mussolini as a puppet leader, in the interests of the Axis. The Italians then concealed Mussolini's whereabouts from the Germans by moving him about.

The scene in a Messina street as a civilian welcomed the arrival of Allied forces in the Sicilian city

On September 12th, Mussolini was rescued from captivity by the Germans. He was then forced, by Hitler, to establish a new fascist regime in northern Italy, named the Italian Social Republic. He remained as puppet leader until April 1945, when he was caught by anti-fascist partisans as he made his way to Switzerland in order to escape to Spain by air. On the 28th he was summarily executed. His body was then hung on display in Milan to satisfy the people that he had got what he deserved, especially for the murder of many Italian partisans.

Mussolini arrested in Rome

Razed to the Ground

In the early hours of the 25th July, 1943, the German city of Hamburg received the first of a series of major bombing raids by the RAF. As the bombers neared their target, they released a cloud of foil strips to confuse radar systems so that the Germans saw only a mass of interference on their screens. Then, in the space of an hour, the British dropped 2,300 tons of bombs across the city. Much of Hamburg was razed to the ground by the bombing, but worse was to come for the inhabitants when the ruined city was engulfed by a firestorm.

It began as a number of small fires left burning after the bombing raid had passed. Conditions happened to be dry, warm and breezy, which allowed the fires to begin spreading. As they met up, there was an exponential increase in heat, so that a conflagration developed. Soon, the convection currents generated by the rising heat were so powerful that air was sucked towards the fire from all directions.

A solitary figure walking through a devastated area of Hamburg, 1944

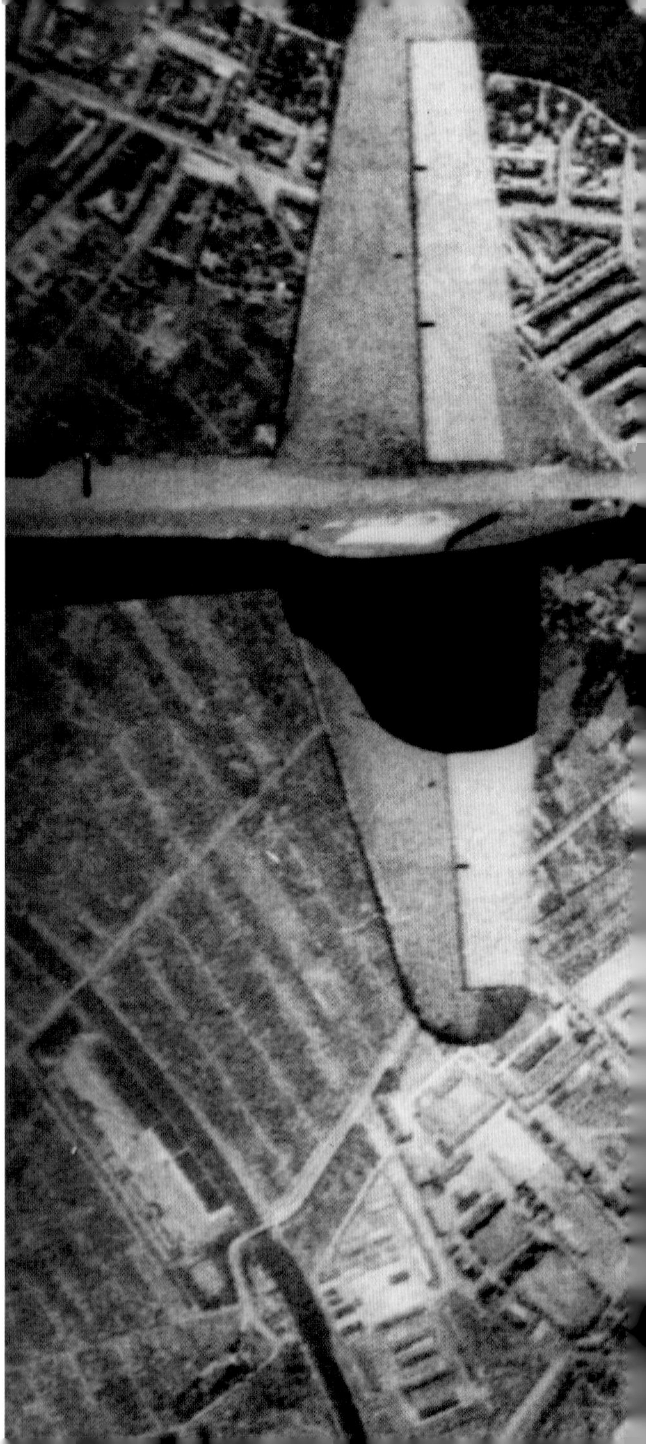

Aerial view of the German city of Hamburg which was heavily bombed by the RAF

The wind was strong enough to suck debris and people into the fire and the surrounding area became so hot with radiation that people were roasted some distance away. Thousands of civilians had been hiding in air raid shelters.

They survived the initial bombing but fell victim to the firestorm by succumbing to heat, hypoxia and carbon-monoxide poisoning. Twenty thousand lost their lives and sixty thousand were hospitalised.

On the 18th November, 1943, it was Berlin's turn to receive a pounding. The intention was a knockout blow to the German home front, but German resistance and tenacity were underestimated.

The bombing campaign lasted until Springtime of 1944, but still the Germans would not relent. Overall, the campaign was judged to have failed because it had not achieved its objective and British losses had been significant. Over a thousand aircraft and seven thousand personnel had been lost, with no perceived gain to the Allies.

A solitary figure walking through a devastated area of Hamburg, 1944

Other German cities targeted with bombs include Bremen and Kiel. Kiel was home to a submarine base, so the bombing was strategically important. Similarly, Bremen was home to German shipyards. The Ruhr industrial region was also subjected to an intense bombing campaign to knock out steelworks, oil processing plants, armament factories and so on.

The bombings lasted from March to July 1943 and greatly hindered Germany's ability to manufacture the equipment and resources it needed for its war effort. It was all part of the attrition needed to ensure that the Allied landings in Italy and France would stand a chance of success.

Soldiers from the Royal Ulster Rifles regiment clear a bombed street as they enter the German city of Bremen

A scene at what was Potsdam Station, Berlin – the station was hit in four heavy bombing raids, two by the RAF and two by the US Air Force

SOLO

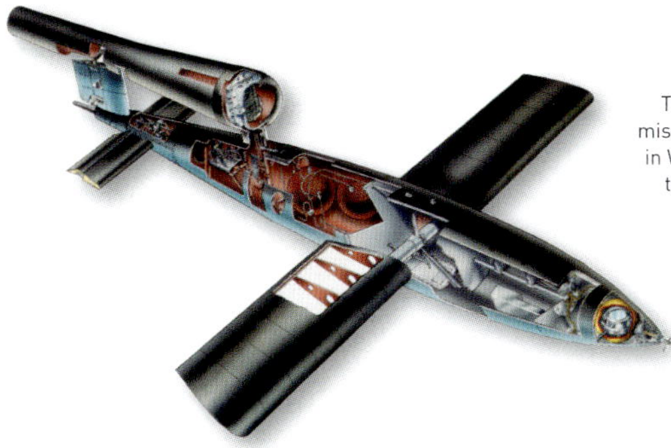

The V-1 was a form of unguided missile developed by the Germans in World War II. It was nicknamed the 'doodlebug', 'or buzz bomb'

Operation Crossbow

Fastidious aerial reconnaissance by British intelligence had revealed that the Germans were developing secret weapons. In 1943 Operation Crossbow was initiated as a counter measure to these developments. Photographs betrayed the existence of mysterious objects and installations in various locations, in Germany and France. At first British command didn't quite know what to make of interpretations of the photographs, because they were taken from above at altitude. There was uncertainty about what the pictures showed, and there was uncertainty about whether they were real or just decoys designed to fool the Allies into launching wasted bombing raids.

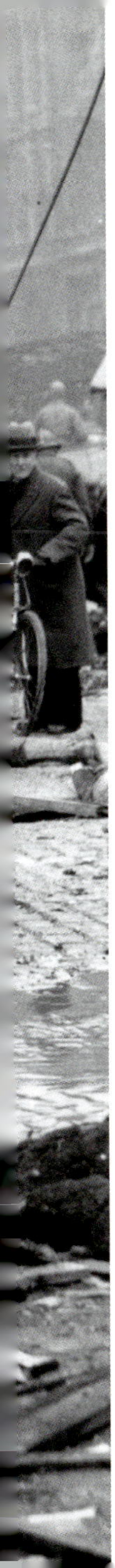

A city street is littered with the corpses of Belgian civilians and soldiers after the explosion of a German V-1 flying bomb

However, images from a site at Peenemünde on the German Baltic coast convinced the Allies that the Germans were indeed working on advanced weaponry. Outlines and shadows suggested flying weapons of one kind or another and indicated that German technology was more advanced than that of the Allies.

The evidence was sufficient to launch Operation Hydra, as part of Crossbow, on the 17th August, which was a strategic bombing raid of the Peenemünde site. The Allies had been correct in their assessment of the evidence, as the site was where the German V-2 Rocket was being prototyped and the V-1 flying bomb was undergoing test flights.

The bombing set developments back and caused the scientists and engineers to relocate, but it also made it clear that the Allies were wise to the V-weapons programmes. In the long-term it meant that the Allies could do little to prevent the V-1 and V-2 from being perfected by the Germans and then being mass produced and used in anger against them.

As Operation Crossbow continued into 1944, attention turned to the launch sites for the weapons, which were being constructed all over north-western Europe. The V-1 used a conspicuous launch ramp and the weapons were housed in hockey-stick shaped sheds, making them fairly easy to spot and destroy. The V-2 was more problematic as it had a longer range and required only a portable launch pad, making it undetectable prior to use. However, the Germans had initially intended to store and launch V-2 rockets from a heavily fortified bunker called La Coupole (The Dome), at the northern tip of France.

It was so heavily bombed by the Allies in the summer of 1944 that the Germans were forced to abandon the site before its completion.

Injured civilians are assisted by rescue workers after a German V-2 rocket exploded in Farringdon Road, London, 1945

After their surrender, a group of German V-2 rocket scientists pose with members of the US 7th Army, 44th Infantry Division, near Oberammergau, Germany, May 2, 1945

Tunisia Campaign

On 13th May, 1943, Winston Churchill received a message, reading "The Tunis campaign is over. All enemy resistance has ceased. We are masters of the North African shores." The news came two months prior to the Allied invasion of Sicily, where the war was about to be taken from Africa to continental Europe. It marked the beginning of the end for the Axis powers.

Before World War II, Tunisia was a French protectorate, with 250,000 French and Italian colonists. It became the last remaining enclave for the Axis powers after a series of North African battles and the Allied campaign to finally defeat the enemy outright began on 17th November 1942.

Initially the combined German and Italian force did well, but the Allies had the logistical advantage. They had open supply lines to keep equipment, provisions and personnel pouring into the theatre of battle, so it was just a matter of time before the Axis force was cornered in the city of Tunis and faced with annihilation or surrender they chose the latter.

German troops after the capture of Tebourba, Tunisia, 1942

BR4
AN V

Some military historians regard the Tunisia Campaign as one of the tactical errors that led to the demise of the Nazi regime. Hitler's motive for sending in so many German troops was to keep the Mediterranean under Axis control, so that an Allied invasion remained impracticable. In reality, it only delayed the inevitable by six months or so and it cost Hitler dearly in terms of available manpower and resources. He would have been better off by evacuating North Africa and consolidating his defences on the European Mediterranean coast.

In hindsight, it is possible that he may have successfully beaten the Allies back from Italy in September 1943, but that is a matter of pure conjecture. After all, he was also in the process of stretching the Axis too far on the Eastern Front. Fundamentally, Hitler's ambitions of conquest got the better of his common sense, because he wasn't guided or motivated by military strategic thinking. He wanted too much too soon, so that he could live up to the promise he had made to the German people and, in his haste to demonstrate his omnipotence, he made basic errors of judgement, so blinded by his ego that he could not listen to the advice offered by his military commanders.

Royal Air Force flying in loose formation over the Tunisian desert providing cover for Allied bombers, April 1943

Pacific Sweep

Following the Battle of Midway, in 1942, the Japanese were limited in their ability to defend their interests, making it easier for the Allies to begin the process of pushing the invaders back towards their own archipelago. Nevertheless, it wasn't going to be an easy process, because Japan's territorial gains comprised a great many islands of different sizes, so that each required its own battle on one scale or another. Also, the Allies would need to mount assaults from sea to land, making them extremely vulnerable to defensive fire while the Japanese were concealed in networks of tunnels, trenches and bunkers on higher ground.

When the Americans began their sweep of the Pacific islands they knew that the holed-up Japanese garrisons were isolated by the retreat of the Japanese force as a whole. This meant it was a matter of attrition in order to take each island. The Americans began by bombarding an island with shells fired from warships placed some distance away, and bombs dropped by aircraft, whilst the landing party prepared to make their assault and establish a beachhead.

View of the USS North Carolina battleship en route in the Pacific Ocean

Despite efforts to destroy enemy positions, the Japanese would often survive in significant numbers and have sufficient weaponry to put up fierce resistance. So, the Americans had to adopt a systematic approach to flushing the Japanese from their lairs. This involved the use of flamethrowers and grenades to either kill or force the Japanese into the open. They were usually shot as they emerged, because they were inclined to have one last attempt at aggression in order to die honourably. Very few surrendered themselves to the Americans, as that was considered such a shameful way to behave.

On the larger islands of Southeast Asia, the situation was rather different, because the theatre of battle was tropical jungle, which presented a different set of problems. In particular, there was the lack of visibility in the thick vegetation. This meant that platoons of Allied and Japanese troops would fall upon one another by chance and enter into battle at close quarters, often involving hand-to-hand combat. In both types of situation, casualty numbers were high, but the Allies gradually and methodically swept the Japanese back to whence they had come. As the circumference of the Japanese held territory reduced however, then the easier it became for them to defend it, so the fighting became progressively more fierce the farther it moved towards the Japanese archipelago.

Japanese kamikaze putting on his forehead bandeau with rising sun, 1944

Infantrymen of the US 8th Army pour ashore in the Subic Bay area of Luzon Island in the northern Philippines, en route to Manila

Anzio and Cassino

In January 1944 the Allies had fought their way up the Italian peninsula to a line above Naples and below Rome, called the Gustav Line. The line ran through the town of Cassino on the route to Rome, which was held by the Germans. The town lay in the shadow of a rocky mount named Monte Cassino, which gave the Germans the advantage of high ground. The Allies were faced with a ferocious battle against the Axis in order to continue their journey northwards.

On the 22nd January, the Allies mounted Operation Shingle, which was a new phase of beach landings on the western Italian coast at Anzio, just above the Gustav Line. This was a strategic offensive designed to present a threat to the Gustav Line from both sides. The Germans were taken by surprise and 50,000 Allied troops had come ashore by the following day. However, the high command were too cautious to venture inland without the delivery of tanks and artillery, and this gave the Germans the chance to reorganize themselves in defence.

American troops dock at the port of Anzio during the Allied invasion of Italy known as Operation Shingle

360

Although the landings were successful in establishing a new foothold on the Italian coast, the ensuing battle turned out to be costly for the Allies. The intention of outflanking the Germans at Monte Cassino was abandoned due to the weight of resistance and the terrain, but the army gradually worked its way north to Rome. This became known as the Anzio breakout, and was made possible by fooling the Germans into thinking that a sea landing would be made near Rome. In anticipation of these landings, German high command redeployed in that area, leaving a point of defensive weakness, which the Anzio troops were able to exploit.

The German 10th Army, which the Allies had hoped to ensnare, ultimately managed to escape the trap by making a fighting retreat northwards, when they realized that Cassino was lost to the Allies. By the time Allied forces reached Rome, the Germans had strategically evacuated the city. In a haunting echo of World War I, the town of Cassino was razed to the ground by shells and bombs, so that it was a field of rubble with the occasional ruin still standing. Above the town, on the mount, there had been a monastery, but it was entirely destroyed by the Allies who mistakenly believed that the Germans had fortified the building in readiness for the battle.

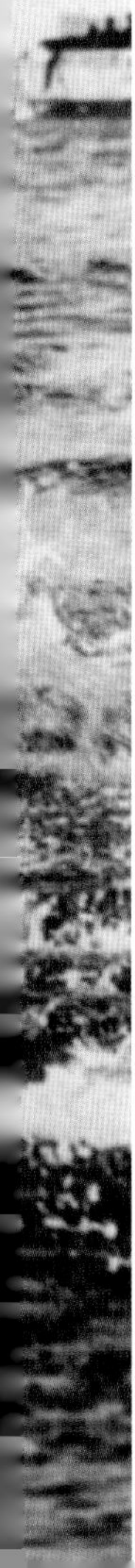

An American soldier landing on the beaches of Anzio, Italy, 50Km south of Rome on January 22, 1944

The Russian War Machine

The turning point for the Eastern Front came with the Battle of Kursk in the summer of 1943. The battle was so costly to the Axis that they were no longer able to prevent the Russians from advancing westward. It had been so costly because the Germans were still in a weakened position following the Russian winter, and they were effectively forced to stand their ground to avoid the advance of the newly optimistic Russians. In anticipation of a German offensive, the Russians had dug themselves into a fortified line, which comprised a remarkable 3750 miles of trenches, nearly a thousand observation and command posts and 48 thousand positions for artillery and mortars.

The Russians had built an impenetrable barrier. They also had 2.5 million troops, while the Germans had less than 1 million and almost 8,000 tanks, to the Germans' 3,000. They also had 2,800 aircraft, while the Germans had 2,100 and they had 25,000 guns and mortars against the Germans' 10,000. Needless to say, the odds were stacked heavily against the Germans from the off.

Battle of Kursk: A German Panzer VI Tiger between Bielgorod and Orel, July 1943

The Russians allowed the Germans to exhaust themselves with the futility of attempting to breach the fortified line and then launched counter-offensives. In terms of losses, the Germans faired far better than the Russians, because they were a far better fighting force, but the battle was a decisive victory for the Russians simply because combative attrition had crippled the German force, which was forced into retreat. Sheer strength in numbers had given the Russians the upper hand, and that is how things remained for the rest of the war.

By the springtime of 1944, the Russians had retaken the Ukraine and were well on their way to pushing the Germans back across Eastern Europe. The Third Reich was steadily retreating from the east and from the south. Soon it would be retreating from the west too, as the Allies were planning a mass invasion of German occupied France, so that Hitler's empire could be eroded from all sides. The Russian army was particularly shocked by discovering the way the Nazis had treated the Russians under their occupation and this resentment grew as they closed in on the regime. Prospects were very grim for any Nazis who were caught by the Russians.

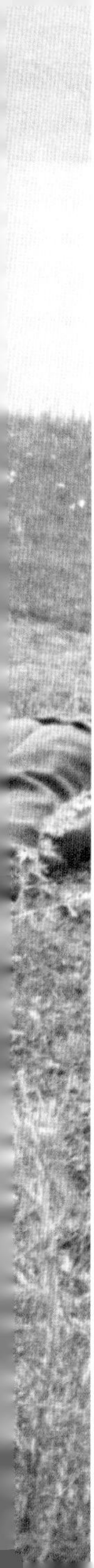

A German soldier sitting with his head in his hands by a destroyed heavy artillery gun following the Battle of Kursk

Plans for Invasion

In order to achieve a successful invasion of Nazi-occupied France, it was necessary for the Allies to organize Operation Overlord in as much secrecy as possible. However, it was impossible to conceal the vast build-up of troops and military equipment necessary for the offensive. This meant that the only real secrets were the time and location of the invasion, so the Allies played this to their advantage.

As the shortest route across the English Channel was between Dover and Calais, the Allies decided to work on the idea that Hitler could be persuaded that this was the intention if they used every trick in the book to deceive him.

Decoy tanks and aircraft were positioned near to the Dover coast to fool German reconnaissance into believing that invasion preparations were underway. Some decoys were fabricated from wood and canvas, others were inflatable rubber, but they appeared very convincing from a bird's eye view. False radio messages were also transmitted, so that German intelligence sent erroneous information to Hitler.

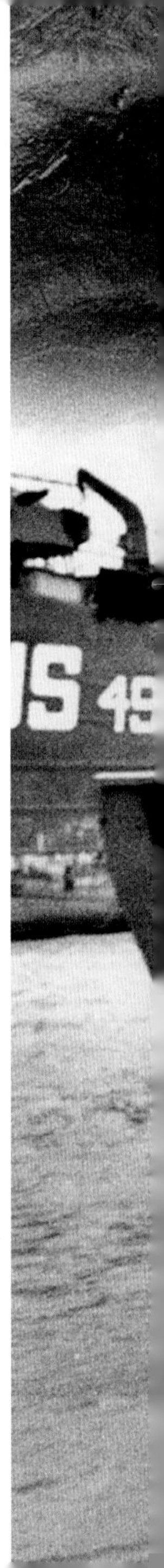

American soldiers disembarking from an LCI landing craft upon its arrival on the beaches of Normandy for Operation Overlord

German Prisoners of War (POW) have been put behind barbed wire on Omaha Beach where American invasion forces landed 6th June, 1944

Meanwhile, efforts were made to conceal the genuine invasion preparation activity going on at or near a number of ports farther to the west on the English south coast. The troops themselves were kept in the dark about the details of the invasion. They were housed at barracks inland, so that they had no idea where they would embark on the final day. The timing of the invasion was not fixed, due to the requirement for clement weather conditions. This meant that everything needed to be able to be held on standby and ready to put into operation at short-notice, as and when high command pressed the green light.

Despite the odds against keeping the plans covert, Hitler remained uncertain about the Allies' plans and decided to keep the majority of his defensive force in the Calais area. When the invasion came in Normandy there was still fierce resistance from the Germans, but nowhere near as much as there would have been had Hitler second-guessed the Allies' plans.

In addition, Erwin Rommel happened to be away on leave, so that German defences were not commanded efficiently. Several Panzer divisions could have been deployed with devastating effect, but Hitler had refused to move them far enough west and Rommel was about to persuade him to do so. As it was, the tanks were too far east, and Rommel was not on the scene quickly enough to orchestrate any measures to prevent the Allies from securing a firm foothold.

D-Day

The first day of Operation Overlord came on 6th June, 1944. It was called D-Day, or Zero-Day, so that each subsequent day had a number: D plus 1, D plus 2, and so on. The idea was that certain objectives were met in rapid succession following the landings, to make sure that Germans were unable to mount a counter offensive and keep the momentum on the side of the Allies.

The landing troops embarked on their journey across the English Channel during the night of the 5-6th June. There had been a storm on the 5th and further storms were forecast, so high command had opted to go for a short window in the weather, rather than wait any longer and risk the Germans finding out.

The beaches of Normandy had been given five code names; Utah, Omaha, Gold, Juno, and Sword, running west to east. The fleet assembled mid-channel, having sailed from various locations in southern England and Wales, and then headed for their fate with destiny.

Soldiers of the 3rd Canadian Infantry Division have set up anti-aircraft guns on Juno Beach where they landed on D-Day

A number of airborne Paratroop units had gone ahead to attack German defensive positions and take bridges near the town of Caen, to prevent the enemy from deploying reserve forces farther west.

When the landing parties began their assaults, they were met with varying difficulties, due to the different geography and defensive installations. Omaha beach, for example, was backed by steep cliffs, with machine gun positions at a vantage point. Troops had to rush to the foot of the cliffs and wait until the defences had been destroyed. Utah beach, as it was farthest west, was only poorly defended.

The troops had relatively little trouble in establishing a safe beachhead. Elsewhere, resistance was fierce, but the Germans were unable to prevent the Allies from coming ashore and defeating them.

Utah and Omaha beaches were assigned to the US First Army. Sword and Gold beaches were assigned to the British Second Army, and Juno beach was assigned to the Canadian Second Infantry Division. By the evening of the 6th, all five beach zones were safely in Allied hands and the armies had met up with the airborne divisions inland.

American soldiers aboard an LCI landing craft on its way across the English Channel towards the beaches of Normandy for Operation Overlord

The next phase of the attack was to consolidate the Allies' position by taking Cherbourg, to the west, and Caen, to the east, before beginning the invasion proper and forcing German lines back towards central Europe.

Meanwhile, there was the matter of supply lines. As the Normandy beaches offered no ports for transport ships to moor up, the Allies used prefabricated floating harbors called 'Mulberries'.

They comprised a floating section that ran out into deep water, so that vehicles could disembark by driving along a gangway and then use ramps to come ashore. In this way, the Allies managed to off-load all of the military hardware and reserve troops they required in a short space of time, to keep the frontline constantly moving.

US troops march up beachhead while landing craft in rear continue to unload supplies, equipment and men following victorious D-Day invasion

US

The Push

On D-Day the Allied force numbered 156,000, while the Germans had just 10,000. By the end of the day, 12,000 Allies had lost their lives against the German defensive positions, but the prime objective of Operation Overlord had been achieved. The Germans lost between and half and two-thirds of their men, while the rest were either taken prisoner or managed to retreat.

The subsequent fight to begin pushing the Germans eastward was not going to be easy. Allied high command had been hopeful of bringing the war to an end before the close of 1944, but the Germans had other ideas. The ceasefire of World War I had seen the Allies and Germans leave the field of battle in France and Belgium. This time, the Germans knew they would be chased all the way back to Berlin, so they put up an incredibly fierce resistance all of the way across Western Europe. Also, as the perimeter of the Third Reich gradually shrank, the German forces had less frontline to defend, so their resistance was undiminishing. As a result, many battles ensued as the Germans made tactical retreats to natural obstacles, such as rivers, where they stood their ground.

German soldiers captured during the Battle of Normandy

Despite their best efforts to keep the Allies from advancing, they inevitably failed because of the same logistical imbalance that had been their undoing on the Eastern Front. The Allies had an inexhaustible supply of equipment and reserve troops, while the Germans had finite and diminishing resources. Of course, the German high command knew very well that the situation was hopeless and wanted to sue for peace before the Allies invaded Germany, but Hitler flatly refused to consider surrender as an option. In fact, it seems that he grew so obsessed with the idea that Germany was 'meant' to win the war, that he wouldn't listen to his military officers. So, the war at the Western Front continued despite the eventual outcome being quite obvious.

In Italy, the Allies had reached the Gothic Line well above Rome. On the Eastern Front, the Russians had entered Poland. It was only a matter of time before Hitler's domain was reduced in size to a smaller area than he had started with. In Asia, the Japanese were being pushed out of China and Burma, and in Southeast Asia they were being steadily purged from the many islands. The wars in both the west and in the east were both going well for the Allies and badly for the Axis.

Soldiers of the 5th Allied Army pass a dead German soldier as they push their way through the enemy's mountainous Gothic line of defence in Italy

V-Weapons

Following the Normandy landings on the 6th June 1944, part of the German's defensive strategy was to unleash their secret weapons, the V-1 flying bomb and the V-2 rocket bomb, in an attempt to make the Allies think twice about advancing.

The first V-1 was launched on the 13th June, just a week after D-Day. Between June and October over 9.5 thousand V-1s were fired at London and other parts of Southeast England. Eventually the launch sites were overrun by the Allies as they advanced eastward, so the Germans were only able to continue firing them at targets in Belgium, because the V-1 had a limited range. 12,000 V-1s were successfully launched, but they killed a relatively low number of civilians, at just short of 23,000. With fewer than two casualties per bomb, they had no persuasive effect on the Allies, but they did have a psychological impact. This was partly because the V-1 was propelled by a noisy pulse-jet engine, which would cut-out to allow the bomb to fall. The abrupt end to the noise struck fear into people, because the exact point of contact with the ground was random, so it was matter of waiting for the sound of the explosion.

The aftermath of a V1 'doodlebug' flying bomb attack, England, 1944

The V-2 rocket bomb was a different matter altogether. It flew at supersonic speed, so no one heard or saw it coming. There would be a sudden and unexpected explosion as the ballistic missile struck the ground from a high trajectory. The first of over 3,000 V-2s was launched on 8th September. They killed an average of about three people, because there was no prior warning of a strike and they carried larger warheads.

The V-1 was essentially an unmanned, or drone, aeroplane. As it was visible, noisy and slow-flying at low altitude, it was fairly easy to shoot down with antiaircraft guns or to intercept with fighter aircraft. The V-2, on the other hand, was state of the art technology and the Allies had no way to counter the threat, apart from preventing it from being launched in the first place. Although the V-2 was a remarkable machine for its time, it was enormously expensive to manufacture. Each V-2 cost the same as a fighter plane, and each V-1 about half that, so Hitler would have been far wiser to have invested in 9,000 aircraft, which would have been far more effective in defending the Western Front.

Canadian soldiers sitting on a German V-1 bomb which failed to reach its target in Britain

Devastation caused by German V1 'doodlebug' in South London, 1944

The Plot Against Hitler

In July, 1944, only the Nazi party faithful still believed that Hitler could win the war. With the Allies back in France and advancing steadily east, most of the German high command knew the game was up. So, they hatched a plot to assassinate the Fuhrer and then negotiate a peace treaty. A number of partisan assassination attempts had failed over the years, as Hitler was careful to make his behaviour varied and unpredictable, but this time it seemed that the plot could not fail.

On the 20th July, a conspirator named Claus von Stauffenberg attended one of Hitler's military conferences, carrying a bomb concealed in a suitcase. Having planted the bomb beneath the table where Hitler would be standing, Stauffenberg was summoned away to a planned telephone call before the blast was detonated. The explosion wrecked the conference room, but Hitler had survived because the wide leg of the table had shielded him from the blast. He was injured, but not mortally, and immediately set about rounding up the conspirators for execution.

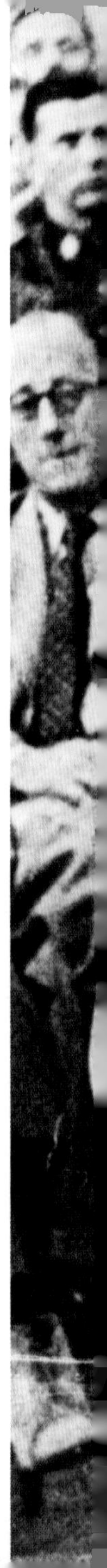

Dr Carl Friedrich Goerdeler, Burgermeister of Leipzig, on trial for his participation in the 'July Plot' to assassinate Hitler

Erwin Rommel, who was blackmailed by Hitler into taking his own life

German General Erwin von Witzleben, who was involved in the July Plot to assassinate Hitler – he was tried, found guilty of treason and hanged in 1944

Meanwhile, the conspirators had been so confident that Hitler must have died in the explosion, that they revealed themselves by prematurely implementing the next stage of their plan. In doing so, they signed their own death warrants, and Hitler had a much better idea of whom he could trust.

Erwin Rommel had agreed to lend his support to the conspiracy against Hitler, which was already afoot in the springtime of 1944. At the time of the bombing, Rommel was recovering from battle injuries, but he was clearly implicated. As Rommel was the most popular officer in the German army, Hitler had a problem to solve. If he had Rommel executed and declared a traitor, then it would cause low morale at the Western Front or even initiate mutiny amongst the army with the knowledge that Rommel had lost faith in Hitler. To avoid a possible coup, Hitler decided to inform Rommel that his family and friends would be murdered unless he committed suicide. So Rommel took a cyanide pill on October 14th 1944. The official version of events was that Rommel had either suffered a heart attack or a brain haemorrhage due to the head injuries he had sustained in July.

Allies at the Gates

On the 29th April, 1945, the German army in Italy surrendered to the Allies. Since the autumn of 1944, the Allied and Axis forces had been in a stalemate, but on the 8th April, 1945, the German frontline began to give way. The Germans made a number of tactical retreats but decided to throw in the towel just three weeks later. This was the start of the closing chapter for the Third Reich.

Only three days prior to the German surrender on the Italian front, the Russians had surrounded Berlin and begun their assault on the German capital, where Hitler and his supporters were holed up. On the 20th April, Hitler had celebrated his 56th birthday, undoubtedly aware that it would be his last. Nevertheless, he resolutely kept on barking orders to the army units defending Berlin, determined that Germany would sink in a ball of flames rather than surrender.

As the Battle of Berlin progressed, the tactics were adapted to street warfare, where every building had to be purged of Nazi resistance. As a result, many civilians died in the crossfire, also, the

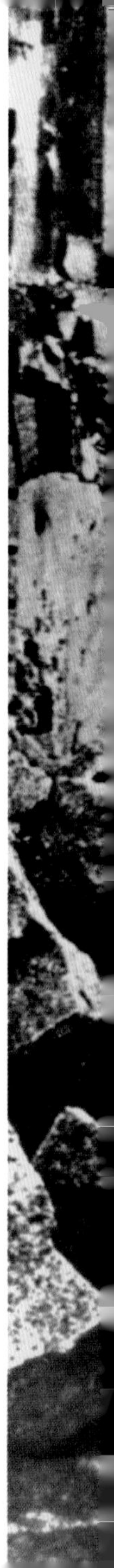

A German soldier sits amongst the ruins of the Reichstag in Berlin after the Russian army entered the city in 1945

MJ 6182

Russians were in no mood to distinguish between the two, as a German was a Nazi in their view. They had seen evidence of the Nazi's inhumanity to man on countless occasions as the Eastern Front had moved west, and sympathy was not much in supply. Many Berlin women were raped by the Russians as a gesture of humiliation and revenge.

When the Nazis realized what they could expect at the hands of the Russians, many travelled west to surrender to the Americans and British, knowing they would have a better chance of survival.

Herman Goering, who had fled to Bavaria, telegrammed Hitler to suggest that he took over the leadership, since the Fuhrer was indisposed and unlikely to escape the Russian encirclement. Hitler was furious but powerless to retaliate. On 28th April, he was informed that his army had only two days' worth of ammunition left, so Hitler resigned himself to his fate. He married his mistress Eva Braun on the 29th and both committed suicide on the 30th. Admiral Karl Dönitz succeeded Hitler until Germany officially surrendered to the Allies on 23 May, 1945.

VE (Victory in Europe) day was celebrated on 8th of May, as that was when hostilities ceased and Allied nations realized that peace had finally arrived after nearly six years of war. However, hostilities had not yet ceased in Asia, where the Japanese were still putting up a spirited and fanatical resistance.

People crowd on top of a van during VE Day celebrations, London, 8th May 1945

Crowds in Piccadilly Circus celebrate VE Day

VERMOUTH VOTRIX
BILE BEANS
ALLEN
YOUR
BUY
SAVINGS
STAMPS

Iwo Jima and Okinawa

As the Americans fought their way nearer to the Japanese archipelago, the enemy battled ever more ferociously. Surrender was not an option for the Japanese mindset, as it was better to die honourably at arms or to commit suicide to avoid the shame of being held prisoner. There was also the incentive of protecting their homeland and the Japanese civilian population. The Japanese army judged the Allies by their own standards and presumed that their people would be harshly treated if they were defeated, so they had every reason to fear their enemy and to fight fiercely to the end. The battles of Iwo Jima and Okinawa have gone down in the annals of history as two of the bloodiest campaigns ever fought.

The Battle of Iwo Jima lasted from February 19th to March 26th 1945. The Allies wanted to take Iwo Jima as a staging post to mount airborne attacks on the Japanese main islands. The prospect of the Americans getting that close to Japan gave the Japanese a resolve that made them very hard to fight.

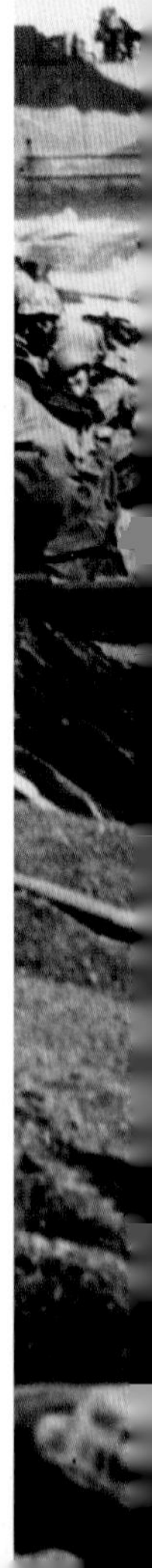

US Marines lying on the beach of Iwo Jima bombarded by Japanese artillery

The Japanese force numbered nearly 22,000 and all died bar just 216 who were taken prisoner. More than 99% of the Japanese troops were killed by the Americans before Iwo Jima was secured. This statistic would be very telling in decisions to come about how to win the war.

It was a similar story with the Battle of Okinawa, fought between April 1st and June 22nd 1945. The Japanese also made use of a kamikaze flying bomb, called the Ohka, which was much like the German V-1, except that it was piloted by a human volunteer, so that it could be aimed precisely at targets, which were usually American ships. The idea of making a certain sacrificing of one's life for the sake of the war effort was alien and disturbing to the Allies, as is indicated a level of fanaticism in the Japanese, suggesting that they would stop at nothing. They also had a kamikaze submarine, called the kaiten, and began using standard aircraft for suicidal bombing missions.

By the time Iwo Jima and Okinawa were in US hands, it was clear that a great many more Americans and Japanese would die if it were necessary to take the war to Japan itself. As the Japanese were not about to surrender or to agree to a ceasefire, the Allies had no choice but to continue their advance until a conclusion was met.

An American serviceman shares his rations with two Japanese children in Okinawa, Japan, 1945

Atomic Bomb

Behind the scenes during World War II, the Allies had grown increasingly concerned that the Nazis and the Japanese might be developing nuclear weapons, for it was known that they were experimenting with nuclear technologies. Unknown to the Allies, the German scientists had abandoned ideas of atomic weapons before Germany surrendered, but the US had initiated a nuclear weapons program in New Mexico, named the Manhattan Project.

On July 16th 1945, the US scientists conducted their first atomic bomb test, called the Trinity Test. It was an unqualified success and it immediately became apparent that the Americans had a terrifying new weapon that might be deployed against the Japanese to end the remaining war in the Far East.

A dense column of smoke rises more than 60,000 feet into the air over the Japanese industrial port of Nagasaki, the result of an atomic bomb

ENOLA
GAY
82

American bomber pilot Paul W. Tibbets Jr. (centre) stands with the ground crew of the bomber 'Enola Gay', which Tibbets flew in the atomic bombing of Hiroshima

The decision to go ahead and use the atomic bomb against Japan was not made lightly and was based on a balance of statistics. It was calculated that a continuation of conventional warfare would kill a quarter of a million Americans and several million Japanese. Although the atomic bomb might kill hundreds of thousands, it was hoped that it would force the Japanese to capitulate, so that overall losses were far fewer.

The first of two atomic bombs was dropped on the city of Hiroshima on August 6th 1945, and was named 'Little Boy'. On detonation, two pieces of uranium were fired together to create a critical mass, leading to nuclear chain reaction and a single explosion with sufficient force to annihilate the entire city.

The second atomic bomb was dropped on the city of Nagasaki on August 9th 1945 and was named 'Fat Man'. This bomb worked on a different principle, which was also used for the Trinity Test. A sphere of plutonium was surrounded by a shell of conventional explosive, so that detonation caused the plutonium to increase in density and initiate a nuclear chain reaction.

The ruins after the atomic bomb attack on Hiroshima

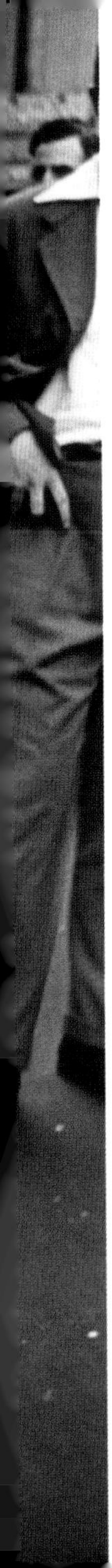

There had been two designs just in case one hadn't worked on the day. In fact, both worked with such devastating effect that the Japanese announced their intention to surrender just five days later. VJ (Victory over Japan) Day was celebrated 14-15th August and the surrender was signed on September 2nd.

It has been estimated that the Hiroshima and Nagasaki bombs killed around a quarter of a million civilians, either in the initial blasts or from injuries and the effects of radiation. It remains a matter of conjecture as to whether that figure would have been exceeded by a conventional conclusion to the war, but it seems likely that it would when considering the Japanese determination to fight or die.

US servicemen celebrate their return home in Time Square following the long awaited-victory over Japan

The Shape of Things to Come

During World War II, the Nazi regime made a systematic attempt to eradicate the Jewish race from Europe. Approximately 6 million Jews died in the Holocaust. When the Allies liberated the death camps, there was universal condemnation of what the Nazis had done. Not least because it became apparent what humans were capable of doing to other humans in the name of ideology and belief. People preferred to think that the savage side of humanity had been left behind in our prehistory. The Nazis showed that it was still there, lying dormant and ready to rear its ugly head when humans were susceptible to the power of suggestion and persuasion.

This collective enlightenment about the true nature of the human condition seemed to generate a reaction against it, in an effort to ensure that the circumstances for its germination never arose again. From this storm of shock and disappointment in humanity came the idea for a Jewish nation, as compensation for their treatment and a way of salving the conscience of the Allies, as much as the defeated Germans, who recognized that anti-Semitism was really the fault of all.

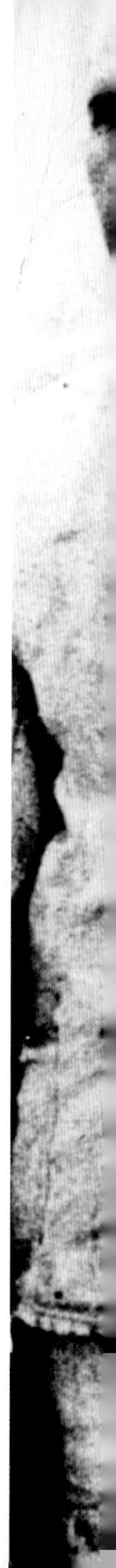

A group of political prisoners held at the Dachau concentration camp by the Nazi's for their opposition to the German regime

So, in 1947 the United Nations General Assembly approved the idea of giving the Jews their own homeland, and in 1948 the State of Israel was formed. Unfortunately, it required the partitioning of Palestine, which displaced another population who had lived there for countless generations. Thus, the Israeli Jews have still never known peace and security, because acquiring the land has led to a whole new set of problems.

As for the Germans, they had to take a long hard look at themselves after the war. Many civilians had either participated in the persecution to some extent, or turned a blind eye to what was going on. There was a general sense of shame that the Nazis had been allowed to take things so far, which led to the unfortunate phenomenon of Holocaust denial. It was easier to deny the truth, despite the overwhelming evidence, by claiming that the evidence was all part of an elaborate conspiracy to discredit the Nazis. That, in itself, provides some idea of just how horrific and unspeakable the Nazi crimes against humanity were.

Following the Nuremburg trials, after the war, many Nazi leaders were executed for their decisions and behavior, which had little or nothing to do with the concept of legitimate warfare, as described by the Geneva Convention. Nazi hunters, bent on revenge and justice, spent decades in pursuit of those Nazis who had managed to escape abroad.

Goering on trial for war crimes in 1946

An Independent World

For different reasons, many European colonies, in Asia and Southeast Asia, began a drive for independence following World War II. For some, it was the feeling that they had sacrificed personnel only because they had been ordered to by the colonial powers and had gained nothing in return. For others, it was because falling under Axis control had not been such a bad experience, as they had been given their autonomy for a few years. As a result the world map began to change considerably in the post-war era.

In marked contrast, other countries lost their autonomy, because they were absorbed into the newly formed Soviet Union. Although the Russians had been among the Allies during the war, this was only a nominal status in real terms. The truth was that the Russians were the enemies of Germany, just as Britain, France and the USA were, but that is where the alliance stopped. Having been the first to Berlin, the Russians wanted a decent sized chunk of Europe as their reward.

Communist-Socialist Bloc meeting, 1947

WARSZAWA
WYZWOLON
17 I
1945
1947

It was difficult to argue against, since the Russians had lost about twenty million people on the Eastern Front, so Stalin got what he wanted. East Germany, Poland, Czechoslovakia, Hungary, Romania and Bulgaria all became satellite states of the Soviet Union, as the Communist Bloc.

Stalin's communist regime then became very internalized and secretive, so that the USA and other Western nations became the Soviet Union's enemies. This state of affairs heightened with the more advanced development of nuclear weapons in the 1950s, so that the Cold War began. In essence, it was a diplomatic stalemate based on the premise of Mutually Assured Destruction (MAD) should a nuclear war ever break out.

This situation perpetuated until 1991, when the Soviet Union collapsed. The countries of the Communist Bloc had their autonomy restored, as did fourteen other nations that had been under Soviet control since 1922. Russia remains the largest country in the world.

India, the single biggest British colony, was granted its independence in 1947. It coincided with the partitioning of the region according to religious differences, primarily Hindu and Muslim so that modern India and Pakistan were created. As the Hindus and Muslims were not neatly divided geographically prior to the partitioning, it resulted in a great deal of ethnic bloodshed as people were forcibly displaced and relocated by the process.

West Berliners peering through the Berlin Wall into the Eastern sector near Check Point Charlie

Picture Credits

All images featured in this book are courtesy of Getty Images © Getty Images.

Page 166: Alfred Eisenstaedt/Pix Inc./Time & Life Pictures/ © Getty Images

Endpapers: front AFP/Getty Images; back Hulton Archive/ © Getty Images

Cover image: Johncairns / © Getty Images